# THE FOUR GOSPELS

## Robert Tremmel

Cover design by Matteo

| Library of Congress Control Number: | | 2010919351 |
|---|---|---|
| ISBN: | Hardcover | 978-1-4568-4262-8 |
| | Softcover | 978-1-4568-4261-1 |
| | Ebook | 978-1-4568-4263-5 |

This book was printed in the United States of America.

**To order additional copies of this book, contact:**
Xlibris Corporation
1-888-795-4274
www.Xlibris.com
Orders@Xlibris.com
92287

# CONTENTS

For Robbie, my first and only love, and
my children, Julie, Heidi and Matthew,
the most special of God's gifts to me.

*All Scripture is inspired by God and useful for teaching,*
*for refutation, for correction and for training in righteousness so*
*that one who belongs to God may be competent and equipped*
*for every good work. (2 Timothy 3:16)*

# PREFACE

Since I was a boy I've had an avid interest in the Bible. In fact, I read the Bible from cover to cover when I was only twelve years old. Not too many people can say that. Perhaps not too many people would want to say that! My dad, even though he rarely went to Church, always read the Bible so, probably in an effort to imitate my father, as boys are apt to do, I started reading it as well. Add to that the fact that my brother was a Trappist Monk who sent me a copy of the then new Knox Bible and you can perhaps understand why a twelve year old would attempt such a task.

I always found the Bible fascinating, not only because of the wonderful stories it contains but also, the mystery therein. After all, we believe it is the Word of God and that God speaks to us through these words so I was anxious to hear what God had to say to me.

My first formal training in Scripture came at the University of Detroit where I studied the Old and New Testament in a theology class. I had a great instructor, Fr. Hodous, a Jesuit who made the Word of God come alive. He was inspiring and encouraged me to read the Bible more often.

However, as I grew older, married and had children, I turned my attention to raising a family and earning a living as a Research Chemist. We went to Church every Sunday but that was the extent of practicing our faith.

Then it happened. For the first time in my life I began to doubt the teachings of the Roman Catholic faith. I even doubted the words of the Scripture I loved so much. I wondered whether Jesus was really raised from the dead, whether there was life after death. I even doubted the existence of God.

Quite frankly, it was a most frightening experience. All my totems were being toppled. Since I was a scientist, my only recourse was to find out the real truth. Surely there must be evidence somewhere. After all, hundreds of millions of people believed the Church's teaching. Many more believed in the

Bible. Many of them were Scholars and Theologians both past and present. They couldn't all be wrong. They must have known things that I didn't know. I started my quest by going back to the Bible that was so important to me as a boy and young man. I read everything about the Bible I could find, which in 1971 was mostly Protestant. Catholic commentaries were available but unless one had access to a Seminary or a Catholic university library, for the average person, they were almost unobtainable. I read everything from ultraconservative to ultraliberal perspectives on the Sacred Scripture. I can honestly say that I read a hundred books in the span of about a year. I was desperate to find out the truth; the meaning behind the mystery so to speak.

One evening, I remember sitting in my favorite chair, reflecting on my year of intense study, and thinking that, in spite of all I had read, I was no closer to the truth than I was when I had started this quest. I was shaken to the core of my being and, holding a Bible in my hands, I prayed, "Oh God, if there is a God, give me the faith to understand the words in this Book." I opened my Bible serendipitously to Matthew, Chapter 5 and began to read the Beatitudes. Now I had read the Gospel of Matthew and the Sermon on the Mount (Matt. 5-7) many times during the course of my life and especially during the past year but I never heard it the way I was hearing it at that moment. It was as though I had never read it before. Suddenly the words were pregnant with meaning. It was as if they were speaking directly to me. Tears welled up in my eyes as I realized for the first time in my life that I had received the gift of faith. During the next few weeks I began to understand that faith was indeed a gift and that a lifetime of study could never replace it. I realized there was a God even though I now knew that no one could ever prove God existed. I realized that wasn't the point. We are called to be a people of faith and we are all on a journey of faith. Believing was far more important than knowing.

However, this doesn't mean that we should remain ignorant, especially ignorant of the Sacred Scriptures. I've learned that the more I knew about the Word of God and the meaning behind the words of Scripture the stronger my faith became. Even when I find that modern scholarship challenges and sometimes contradicts the conventional understanding of the sacred text, instead of shaking my faith, this newer knowledge helps me to see things from a different perspective and often strengthens my faith.

After that experience I became more involved in the Church. My wife, Robbie, and I became co-directors of the youth group at St Roch's Church in Flat Rock, Michigan. The pastor there, a wonderful priest named Larry

Dunn, realized my love for the Scriptures, and asked if I would teach a bible class for the people of the parish. I was needless to say, flattered, especially since, except for that theology class at the University of Detroit, I had had no formal training in Sacred Scripture.

Those classes marked the beginning of what has now been more than thirty five years of teaching Scripture on a parish and vicariate level. In between, I was ordained a Permanent Deacon in 1980. After that, I continued my studies, focusing primarily on The New Testament, by taking graduate classes at St John's Major Seminary in Plymouth, Michigan and Sacred Heart Major Seminary in Detroit, Michigan.

This book is the result of the many classes I have taught. It is primarily taken from notes for presentations I have made on the four Gospels at St Joseph's Catholic Community in Trenton, Michigan and also a Jesus seminar I recently gave in my assigned parish, Sacred Heart Catholic Community in Grosse Ile, Michigan.

The positive response to those classes and the support I have received from those who attended them has inspired me to write this book. It is my hope that you will be inspired, not so much by what I write, but by the written word that we call the four Gospels.

I think it's important to prepare for the chapters in this book by reading the selected Gospel beforehand. I prefer that you use the New American Bible (NAB) as it is the one that I will be quoting. However, there are many excellent translations that are available. Aside from the NAB, I recommend the Revised Standard Bible, The New King James Bible, The New Revised Standard Bible or the Good News Bible. All four are modern translations, which are very close to the sense of the original texts. The New Revised Standard Bible uses inclusive language so the translation has been compromised a bit.

I suggest you read the Gospel that will be discussed from beginning to end. If the bible you are using has introductions to the books, be sure to read them first. Pay particular attention to the footnotes as you read. Keep your Bible handy so that you can refer to the passages and texts I highlight.

Ideally, you can read this book with someone else so that you can discuss what you have read with that person. Hopefully, after reading this book, you will have a greater appreciation for the Scriptures and in particular the four Gospels.

# INTRODUCTION

It amazes me that Christians know so little about the Bible. Some, especially Fundamentalist Christians, can quote the Scripture word for word, but for many of them, the Word of God seems frozen in time, separated from its original context. For them, every word in the original Greek and Hebrew seems to have an exact English equivalent. Not only were the sacred authors inspired but the translators of the King James or the Revised Standard versions were inspired as well; or at least they would have to be for the English equivalent to be the Word of God. Many Catholics are bible illiterate. They can recall some of the readings from their Sunday liturgies but most wouldn't know whether Hebrews or Ephesians was from the Old Testament or New Testament! Others, who call themselves Christians, but rarely attend Church services, may not even know that the Old Testament and New Testament are derived from two different traditions or that the Epistles are found only in the New Testament. Many think that the Bible is composed of two books, the Old Testament and the New Testament. In reality it is a library of books: 39 or 46 books in the Old Testament or Hebrew Scriptures as they are now called[1], and 27 books in the New Testament or Christian Scriptures.

---

[1]   The number of books in the Hebrew Scriptures is different because Catholics recognize seven more books as inspired than Protestants. This is because the Catholic Church used the Septuagint, the Greek translation of the Old Testament made in the 3rd century BCE. They chose to do this because all the Old Testament Scripture quoted in the New Testament is only from the Septuagint. Protestants follow the Jewish Canon, known as the Masoretic Text, which was established in the second century CE. The more modern translations of Protestant Bibles add the extra books and even some others from the Septuagint that are not listed in the Catholic Bible. They usually

Add to this the fact that the books of the Bible are, for the most part, quite different from each other. This is because they comprise a wide variety of literary genres. The Book of Genesis, for instance contains both sacred myth and epic history. The Psalms are songs and Proverbs are, as you might have guessed, proverbs. The Book of Job is drama and perhaps was actually dramatized on stage by Greek speaking Jews a few hundred years before Christ. The Christian Scriptures contain perhaps one of the most unique literary genres, "Gospel". Then there are letters, e.g. Paul's epistles, apocalyptic, e.g. Revelation and salvation history, e.g. Acts. Within these books we also find numerous literary forms. For example, there are miracles, epiphanies, allegories and parables to name a few.

As you can see, treating the Bible as a one-dimensional piece of literature does great injustice to the text. To view the four Gospels that way, in my opinion, would even be a greater crime. We all need to understand that the Bible is a multifaceted literary masterpiece, which has many layers of meaning. So, we're not going to do that. We are going to examine the text and try to uncover several layers of meaning if need be and also try to determine the context in which the Gospels were written.

Since this book is not meant to be a scholarly commentary, for the most part, I'm going to primarily examine the Gospels thematically. In other words, what was the basic premise or premises that the sacred author had in mind when he or she wrote it? What was the backdrop behind a particular Gospel? Everyone writes for a reason. Certainly there were issues that needed to be addressed.

There was a Christian community in which the sacred author lived. I think it's safe to assume that he or she is addressing the needs and problems of his or her community. Finally, can we determine the context in which a particular Gospel or story in the Gospel was written? This is extremely important because anything that is taken out of context will rarely, if ever, reflect its true meaning.

I also do not plan to use references. Books on Scripture normally have copious references. Personally, I find them distracting. While there are numerous footnotes used to add to or clarify a point, there are no references since I am only referring to class notes and outlines which are solely my own. I'm certain I referred to books and dictionaries while putting together

---

fall under the heading of "The Apocrypha". The extra books in the Catholic Bible are: *Tobit, Judith, The Book of Sirach (Ecclesiasticus), Baruch, The Book of Wisdom, and 1 and 2 Maccabees.*

my presentations, however, everything was put into my own words so this book is totally in my words, not someone else's.

Studying the Scriptures is a great adventure. So, we are going on a quest, a journey that hopefully will uncover many layers of meaning for us; knowledge that will help us on our journey of life and especially our journey of faith. After all, that's why the Bible was written: to reveal God and God's plan for mankind and to provide a guide for right living.

## BIBLICAL INTERPRETATION

People, who have never studied the Bible, have a tendency to take every word contained within it literally. Some Christian denominations still translate the Bible in this way although, more recently they're beginning to use some historical-critical analysis. I will address this later. I'd like to think that, while the Bible is inspired by God, God allowed its many authors the freedom to express God's word in their own way. This means they were free to use the language and idiomatic and colloquial expressions familiar to them. Their narratives were shaped by their own personal experiences and conditioned by the society in which they lived. What I'm saying here is that God is not concerned with the tools of literary expression. God is only concerned with Revelation. Most Christian denominations believe that everything we need to know for the salvation of our souls is found in the Bible. The literary form used to present it is up to the Sacred Writer.[2]

Perhaps I can make this easier to understand by using the Book of Isaiah and the Letters of St Paul as examples. Most scholars believe that parts of Isaiah were not written by Isaiah and that of the 13 letters of Paul only seven were actually written by Paul. What is now called "Two and Three Isaiah" i.e. the last third of the Book of Isaiah was actually written by disciples of Isaiah and disciples of the disciples of Isaiah, for the most part, long after Isaiah was dead.

Likewise, most experts now believe that disciples of Paul also wrote the six contested letters of Paul after Paul died. In our socio-cultural milieu,

---

[2] This method of biblical interpretation is authorized by the Roman Catholic Church and is presented in detail in the "Dogmatic Constitution on Divine Revelation" which is often found in the beginning of "The New American Bible".

we would call them forgeries but for the ancient people of the Middle East this practice was common. They considered it a way to honor that person plus they believed that the person's spirit inspired them and so, in this way, continued to find expression through their words.

The same can be said of the inspired Word of God we call the Bible. While God allowed the sacred author a great deal of literary freedom, the Holy Spirit was present so that those words would reveal God and express God's will for mankind. As far as God was concerned it didn't matter if the sacred author used drama, poetry, narrative or parables to express that. In fact, it seems to me that narrative, especially historical narrative, would fall far short of expressing something as subjective and profound as God's will!

Now, once we accept the fact that the Bible is a piece of literature, we have to admit that it is subject to examination as such. This doesn't mean that anyone is trying to prove that the Bible is not the inspired Word of God. What it does mean is that modern tools of literary interpretation can be applied so as to better understand the context in which a particular bible story was written and hopefully the meaning that the author had in mind when he or she wrote it.

The scholar then, to do his or her work properly, must be objective in his or her approach and report conclusions in the same vein. This is a scientific approach and, in order to draw accurate and responsible conclusions, faith must be set aside. One's findings can then be reported in light of the person's faith but not as a result of faith.

While I don't want to discuss the modern tools of biblical interpretation in detail, here is a list of the most important ones with a brief explanation:

1) Literary Criticism: A detailed analysis of the components and structure of the biblical text, e.g. rhythm, word choice, style, etc.
2) Textual Criticism: Compares various manuscripts to determine the oldest and most probable rendering.[3]

---

[3] There are ten well known manuscripts dating from the fourth century which contain all four Gospels and there are eight major papyri which contain large sections of the some of the four Gospels. These papyri date from the late third century to the seventh century. There are some small fragments of papyri, which predate the third century, and contain a verse or a few passages of a Gospel. It might surprise many that there are no extant original versions of any of the Gospels nor are there any available first, second, third or even seventh generation copies.

3) Form Criticism: Compares the literary form to similar forms of expression used during the same time period. For example, Paul's letters use the literary form of "letter" commonly used in the first century Greco-Roman world.

4) Source Criticism: Determines the original source(s) of the books of the Bible. For example, it is apparent that Matthew and Luke used Mark as their primary source plus an unknown document or oral tradition that contained the sayings of Jesus.

5) Redaction Criticism: Determines if the text was edited and, if so, why? For example, using this method it becomes obvious that the Gospel of John was edited more than once.

6) Historical Criticism: Compares artifacts and even other writings from the time as well as information in the text itself, which is then used to verify the date of composition and the contents. For example, the methods used for crucifixion, as describe in documents from outside the New Testament, verify that the crucifixion narrative regarding Jesus is quite accurately portrayed.

Biblical literary criticism offers us a much more in-depth and balanced view than a monographic approach. The recognition of various literary forms of expression helps us to develop a greater appreciation for the written word that we call Sacred Scripture. It should also make us aware that we need guidance if we are to properly understand it. We cannot properly interpret it on our own.

However, this does not preclude personal reflection or the reading the Scriptures for personal edification and spiritual growth.

## THE GOSPELS

The Gospels are certainly the most important part of the New Testament. Using the various forms of literary criticism mentioned above, scholars have opened up a whole new understanding of the books we call Mathew, Mark, Luke and John.

There are those who read the Bible regularly but never see the many contradictions that these texts contain. Indeed, there are many areas where the texts do not agree. How can they be reconciled or can they be reconciled? Some would be surprised to discover that they are different for a specific reason and just because, for instance, Luke's infancy narrative contradicts

Matthew's doesn't mean that one or the other is not the Word of God. Modern scholarship teaches us that they don't have to be reconciled to be the Word of God.

Others, who interpret the Bible literally, often try to get around the contradictions or perhaps even ignore them. Matthew 11:11 is one instance that stands out against a literal interpretation. Here Jesus says, "Amen I say to you, among those born of women there is none greater than John the Baptist." For those who translate the Bible literally this is a provocative statement since it demands one to ask if John the Baptist is greater than Jesus! Since Jesus was born of a woman the literalist must conclude that John the Baptist is indeed greater than Jesus which, of course, cannot be true.

Contrarily, if one takes this phrase in context with what follows, along with other Scripture, it becomes quite easy to determine what Matthew's Jesus is saying. The phrase concludes with the words, "yet the least in the kingdom of heaven is greater than he." Jesus is saying that John belongs to the Old Testament/Covenant which is steeped in Torah, i.e. Hebrew law. Among the Prophets of Israel he is the greatest, however, those who accept the Gospel and are baptized enter the kingdom of heaven and therefor are greater than he. John 3:3-5 tells us that to enter the kingdom of heaven one must be born again of water and the Holy Spirit. John the Baptist was born of a woman; the true followers of Jesus are reborn from above and, as a result become as Paul would say, "a new creation in Christ" (See Galatians 6:15). Therefore, even the least in the kingdom of heaven would be greater than John.

If we understand that the Gospels are not a biography of Jesus Christ many of the problems with agreement disappear. Think about this. The Gospels only deal with a year or two of the ministry of Jesus; they tell us almost nothing of his childhood or even his early adult life. We don't even know what Jesus looked like! Obviously, they are not meant to be biographies. The very word "Gospel" means that we are not dealing with biography. Mark uses the Greek word *euangelion*, which literally means "good news". The word means something that is proclaimed orally rather than written. A good image is the town crier walking down the street shouting out the news of the day.

So "Gospel", by its very nature, is something that, at least initially, was not a written tradition. It's a proclamation of the Jesus event, which means it's not only about the Jesus of history, but also the risen Jesus who continued to be present in the earliest Christian communities through the presence and power of the Holy Spirit. In fact, as we shall see later, the risen Jesus is actually more responsible for the four Gospels than the Jesus of history.

However, there are some scholars and Church leaders who tend to mythologize the Gospels. Some have gone so far as to say the Jesus of history is not presented in the Gospels at all; that the Jesus of the Gospels was fabricated by the Christian Communities. As a result, we can never know what Jesus really said or did if there really was a Jesus! While I would agree that in many instances we don't have the exact words of Jesus and his deeds have been somewhat altered or changed by the sacred writer to make a point, we are still in good hands so to speak. I say this because there are too many instances in the Gospels that would not be there if they were contrived or if the sacred authors deliberately tried to falsify the traditions handed on to them

Let me give you some of the many examples. If the evangelists were trying to fabricate a believable story about Jesus, why would they have John baptize him? The one who baptizes was thought to be superior to the one who is baptized. Why not leave this tradition out? As another example, all the Gospels present Jesus as being at odds with his family. In Mark they think he's gone mad (3:21). In John we are told his brothers didn't believe in him (7:5). In all the Synoptic Gospels the people of Jesus' hometown as well as his kin reject him (Mk 6:1-6, Matt. 13:55-58 et al). I would think that if one were trying to make a case that Jesus is the Messiah and the Son of God he or she wouldn't want this part of the story in his or her Gospel. Another important matter is the fact that women are the first to report that Jesus was raised from the dead. Women of that era were not considered reliable witnesses. Their testimony was not acceptable in a court of law. Why would the evangelists record this? For me, the answer to these questions is that the Sacred Writers were trying to record the traditions which were handed down to them as accurately as possible.

As I stated above we have to remember that even though we have discrepancies and contradictions this does not mean that what we are reading is not the Word of God. As we shall see, each Evangelist has an agenda. What he or she is writing is an interpretation of the traditions received in light of the issues that are present in his or her community. I believe that each evangelist has been as faithful as possible to those traditions. There has been no attempt to deceive or mislead the reader.

# GOSPEL FORMATION

You may be surprised to find that the Gospels are not the oldest writings in the New Testament. Most scholars believe that our earliest Gospel, the Gospel of Mark, was written around 70 **C.E.**[4]. This is, at least twenty years after Paul wrote his first letter to the Thessalonians. In fact, if Paul authored all of his letters, every one of them was written prior to the Gospel of Mark. Since the rest of the Gospels were written twenty to thirty years after Mark, their testimony regarding Jesus is a generation or two removed from the life of Jesus. In addition, as far as we can tell, all four Gospels were influenced by Greek culture. They were written in common Greek (called *koine*) and they all used the Greek translation of the Old Testament (called the Septuagint) as a source. The relatively late dates for the composition of the four Gospels means the Christian community had time to reflect on the words and deeds of Jesus. As such, they interpreted them in light of their current situation.

So the Gospels are not a word for word description of the life of Christ or even his ministry. Rather they are a proclamation of the Christ event, which draws from his historical life, plus an interpretation of what his life and deeds meant to the Christian communities of the first century. Not only are they an expression of the words and deeds of the historical Jesus but also, as I mentioned earlier, an expression of the risen Christ who continued to be present in the Christian community. You will have a much better understanding of this concept when we get to the Gospels of Matthew and John.

As I said above, the letters of Paul are the first extant written testimony about Jesus. There may have been other writings which date earlier than Paul's letters but, if there were, we are not aware of them. It's possible that part of the Didache, an early Church training guide, may be pre-Pauline but there is not a lot of evidence to support this. So Paul is almost certainly our earliest known source. However, Paul focuses on the Christ event rather than the historical Jesus. He wants to show us philosophically and theologically that Jesus' death on the cross was salvific, i.e. he suffered and died for the sins of mankind, and if we believe this we are put right with God which basically means we will go to heaven. Regarding the life of Christ, he only tells us that he was born of a woman, that he was betrayed by one of his

---

[4]    "**C.E.**" means "The Common Era". "**B.C.E.**" means "Before the Common Era" In the age of political correctness Scholars now use them as a replacement for "**B.C.**" and "**A.D.**".

own disciples, that he had a brother named James, that he suffered and died on the cross, rose from the dead and appeared to several individuals as well as a large group of about 500 people (See 1 Cor.15: 3-8). Except for the resurrection appearances he offers us very little detail about Jesus' life and ministry. For instance, he never tells us Jesus was a miracle worker or he cast out demons and, except for one instance, he doesn't tell us anything that Jesus said which can be found in the Gospels. The one instance is in 1 Corinthians 11 where he gives us the words of consecration at the Last Supper, which is similar to those found in the Synoptic Gospels.

So, if we only had Paul's letters as a source we would know very little about Jesus. Fortunately, we have four other testimonies—the four Gospels. But where did the Gospels come from? How did they come into existence? Are they biographies, theological treatises, a combination of both or are they something else?

Some naively think that Jesus dictated the Gospels to the Twelve Apostles before he died; others think that an angel whispered the words into the ears of the Evangelists. Still others think that the Apostles were taking notes while Jesus was talking and doing his thing so to speak. In the last instance, nothing could be further from the truth. I say that with a great deal of confidence because it is likely that most, if not all of the disciples, would have been illiterate. Writing materials were very expensive and people dedicated their whole lives to learning how to effectively write. There were no steno pads or ballpoint pens. Quite frankly, the likelihood that anyone wrote anything down while Jesus was alive or even shortly after his death is very remote.

So, what really happened? No one knows for sure, however, the most likely scenario is that, after the resurrection and the coming of the Holy Spirit, the followers of Jesus, especially the Twelve, began to proclaim Jesus was the Messiah, he worked signs and wonders, was crucified, but God raised him from the dead and soon he would come to establish a kingdom here on earth. They swore this was true and that they themselves witnessed the presence of the risen Jesus. This is basically a recap of Peter's sermon on the day of Pentecost as described by Luke in Acts 2:22-24. Even though Acts was written many decades after Peter preached this sermon we can be reasonably certain that he spoke words similar to these. I say this because not only does this sermon have an Aramaic flavor indicating an early tradition but also is repeated several times by both Peter and Paul. Some additional details are added with each ensuing sermon, which may give of us a clue about how the Gospels were formed.

Initially, these basic facts were preached to those who lived in and around Jerusalem. There was no need to add much detail because those who lived in Judea had certainly heard of Jesus and many had probably seen him. Acts tells us that the Gospel spread to Samaria and Galilee and that during Paul's persecution of the Church many believers went to Damascus in Syria. Those in Galilee and Samaria also knew about Jesus and certainly many would have seen and heard him; however, once the Gospel spread to regions outside of Palestine the apostles would have had to add more detail to their message. It is apparent from Acts and Paul's letters that a Christian community was established in Antioch, Syria as early as 40 **C.E.** and in Rome before 50 **C.E.** These people never heard of Jesus and mere curiosity demanded that the Gospel message needed to be expanded. It would be natural to ask questions about what Jesus said about divorce, sexual mores, details about the Kingdom of Heaven, what is required to be a disciple and so on. Jesus was a storyteller so they would want to hear those stories. He was a miracle worker and they would have asked the apostles and other eyewitnesses to tell them about his miracles.

In the process of addressing these questions each apostle or group of disciples would develop a Gospel tradition, which would naturally be unique. We know about four of these traditions: Matthew, Mark, Luke and John. There certainly must have been more since there were many apostles plus disciples who were not among the Twelve.[5] I also think that these traditions were probably oral rather than written. I say this because it seems evident from "Acts" and the letters of Paul that the earliest followers of Jesus believed that he was going to return and establish his kingdom during their lifetime. As a result, at least during the first twenty years after the resurrection, they would not have felt a need to write anything. The only exception may have been a simple missionary guide to maintain some consistency in their basic teaching.[6]

---

[5]     Paul always refers to the Apostles as "The Twelve". There were others known as apostles. They were simply evangelists who spread the Gospel. To qualify one had to either be with Jesus since the beginning of his ministry or saw him after he rose from the dead. Paul tells us the Jesus appeared to 500 people so many would qualify to be an apostle in this broader sense.

[6]     This document may have been what is known as the Didache or "The Teaching of the Twelve Apostles". Parts of the Didache appear to be very early, perhaps dating to the time of Paul's first letters. It includes a basic moral guide called "The Way" which contains some of the "Sermon on the Mount" material in

As I mentioned above the Gospel of Mark seems to be the earliest known Gospel. When I refer to the four Gospels I mean the four Gospels in the form in which we have them today. There may well have been earlier versions of Matthew, Mark and Luke. Many scholars are certain that there was a primitive form of the Gospel of John, which served as a basis for Canonical John. We do not have any record of these Gospels but I think it makes sense to say that the Gospels were generative. For example, even though all four of our Gospels were written in common Greek, Mark betrays an Aramaic author and, as a result, contains a lot of Semitic phrases and expressions. Parts of Matthew can easily be translated into Aramaic indicating that the author may have used an earlier Hebrew or Aramaic source[7]. Luke's author states in his/her prologue that, "many have undertaken to write down the words and deeds of Jesus". If Luke's Gospel was written in about 62 **C.E.**, as Acts indicates, who are these "many"? None of the three other Gospels were written before about 70 **C.E.**! However, if Luke's Gospel was edited and/or redacted near the end of the first century there would have been many other Gospels.

All this is supposition. We have no concrete evidence of these earlier Gospels. However, Papias, a Church Father, writing in the second century, states that Matthew wrote down the sayings of Jesus in the Hebrew language.[8] Canonical Matthew was written in Greek not Hebrew. It also contains a lot more than the sayings of Jesus. However, the words of Papias at least imply that there was a collection of Jesus sayings written by Matthew in Hebrew, which, if indeed Matthew the Apostle wrote them, most likely predated all four Gospels.

None of the four Gospels have a signature or a date of composition. Nor do we have any of the originals. In fact, the oldest complete texts of all four Gospels only date back to the late fourth century.[9] So how do we know who

---

Matthew. It also contains guidelines, which were probably added later, for celebrating the sacraments of Baptism and Eucharist as well as roles for Church leaders.

[7] Aramaic was a Semitic language commonly spoken in Israel, Syria and Mesopotamia from around 500 B.C. to about 500 A.D. Hebrew was only spoken in Israel during liturgical services and in government meetings.

[8] Papias was the second century Bishop of Hierapolis who is quoted by Iranaeus, the second century Bishop of Antioch, as a man who knew John the elder (the apostle?) and was a friend of Polycarp, the first century Bishop of Smyrna.

[9] The two sources are the Sinaitic Manuscript found by Tishendorf in the nineteenth century at the Monastery of St. Catherine in the Sinai Peninsula

wrote them and when they were written? The answer is we do not know for sure. The early Church Fathers are our earliest link to the Gospels and their authors. Papias is the first to refer to the Gospels and his remarks are not firsthand. They are recorded many years later by Eusebius who, in his Ecclesiastical History, is quoting Iranaeus. How accurate is his rendition? Some, if not many, scholars question it. However, it is still a testimony that must be taken seriously since it is the earliest known testimony regarding the Gospels.

---

and the Latin Vulgate, a text translated from the original Greek by St Jerome in the early fourth century.

# Chapter One

# THE GOSPEL OF MARK

As far as we can tell Mark is the inventor of the literary genre we call "Gospel". His opening words state, "This is the Gospel (literally "good news") of Jesus Christ the Son of God" (Mark 1:1). As mentioned above, Gospel is something that is proclaimed and derived from an oral tradition. As far as we can tell, Mark is the first to put this oral proclamation on paper—in this case papyrus. In a sense, this opening line tells us Mark's objective. He wants to show his audience that Jesus is the Christ, which means the anointed one of God, and that he is a King. The phrase "Son of God" is not a divine title for Mark. Every Jewish male was deemed a son of God but only the King of Israel was call *the* Son of God.[10] Mark 15:26, which can be read as a fulfillment of Mark's opening line, has the Romans name Jesus "King of the Jews". While this is the major theme in Mark, we shall see that this Gospel is far more complex.

Even though Matthew is always listed first and, as such, was deemed to be the first Gospel written, modern scholarship believes that Mark preceded not only Matthew but Luke and John as well. The main reason for this is that substantial portions of Mark are found in Matthew and Luke. Of the 660 verses, which make up the Gospel of Mark, 600 are found at least in part in the Gospel of Matthew. Almost 60% of Mark is found in the Gospel of Luke. Many verses are word for word indicating the both Matthew and Luke had a copy of Mark in front of them when they were writing their

---

[10]  Some manuscripts omit "the Son of God" indicating there may have been an earlier version of Mark which only focused on Jesus as the Messiah of Israel.

Gospels. Matthew and Luke also follow Mark's general outline, which begins with the baptism of John, followed by the temptation in the desert, then signs and wonders intermingled with some teaching. All conclude with the Passion and the empty tomb on Easter Sunday.

These three Gospels are called the Synoptic Gospels because; if they are placed side by side in parallel columns all similar texts can be read in a single glance. The Greek word for this is *synopsis*. One will find that if the texts are laid out along side of each other they contain a lot of the same material.

## WHO WROTE IT?

Papias said that Mark was Peter's interpreter and wrote down the words and deeds of Jesus as best he could remember them but not necessarily in the order in which they occurred. This Mark is deemed to be John Mark who is mentioned in Acts and the letters of Peter and Paul. These documents tell us that he was a cousin of Barnabas and a disciple of both Peter and Paul. Another tradition says that he was the son of Mary the wife of Cleopas who is mentioned in the Gospels. Still another tradition says that Cleopas was the brother of Joseph the paternal father of Jesus so this John Mark would be a cousin of Jesus, albeit a step cousin. In spite of these connections, the author of Mark's Gospel was not very familiar with Galilee and the region around the Sea of Galilee. Peter lived in Galilee most of his life. He would have certainly been very familiar with the geography of the Sea of Galilee, and one would expect that the primary source of this Gospel would have accurately described the environs of an area where he grew up and lived. However, Mark could be using this geography theologically rather that historically so I still believe Peter is the primary source of this Gospel. I also say this because Matthew and Luke held this Gospel in such high esteem that they used it as their primary source. John Mark certainly wouldn't have commanded such respect unless he was transmitting the words of someone with notoriety. Peter would certainly be such a person.

## DATE OF COMPOSITION

It's likely that Mark was Peter's scribe and, as such, may have written a proto Gospel in his own Aramaic language. This Gospel would have been quite brief and was probably written around 50 **C.E.** Clement of Alexandria is quoted as saying that Mark wrote his Gospel in Alexandria in about the middle of the first century. If this is true, I think that Gospel was edited and translated into Greek, either by Mark or someone else between 65 and 75 **C.E.** I posit this scenario because the Greek in Mark is very poor indicating that Greek was not the author's primary language. Mark fits this description. Also, as I stated above, someone of great importance would have to stand behind this Gospel for both Matthew and Luke to use it as a primary source. The original Gospel may have simply been a collection of some of the deeds of Jesus, as told by Peter, with a primary emphasis on his passion and death. Canonical Mark is a theological masterpiece that was occasioned by the situation in Mark's community to which it is addressed. Many scholars believe that the community is this case was Rome. It is important to understand the socio-political and religious milieu in both Rome and Jerusalem between 65 and 70 **C.E.** to know the context in which Mark was written.

## BACKGROUND

Around 65 **C.E.** the emperor Caesar Nero burned the city of Rome so that he could start an ambitious building program. When rumors began to circulate that indeed he had set the fires, he blamed them on the Christians. A fierce persecution of the Christian community in Rome ensued, which resulted in the martyrdom of many including Peter and Paul. Some of the Christians denied their faith and some even betrayed their fellow Christians. Shortly after the persecution began, rebel Jews known as Zealots, drove the Romans out of the City of Jerusalem, secured the city and called for divine intervention to deliver the Jews from Roman rule. In 70 **C.E.** the Romans breached the walls of the city, killed most of its inhabitants and destroyed the Temple.

These events had a dramatic effect on all Christians but especially those in Rome. The persecution caused havoc within that community because, while those who stood up to the Emperor became food for the lions, others denied their faith and some even turned in their brethren to escape punishment. The situation in Jerusalem had a dramatic effect on them as well. Many of the Christians in Rome were Jewish. Jerusalem and the Temple had been the center of Jewish worship since the days of Solomon (950-900 **B.C.E.**). This was God's city and it was apparent to them that all these events were a sign that Christ was going to return to establish his kingdom. After all Jesus had predicted that catastrophic events would take place prior to his return.

Once the persecution in Rome ended they faced other issues. They had to decide how to deal with apostates who wanted to return to the faith. They had to decide what they were going to do without the leadership of the likes of Peter and Paul. And, if Jesus was going to return soon they had to prepare for his return. It was against this backdrop that the Gospel of Mark was written.

## HIGHLIGHTS AND THEMES (1-14:21)

Mark is divided into two main parts. The first part focuses on Jesus' ministry of healing and his preaching in Galilee, which serves to prove that he is the Messiah. The second part focuses on the meaning of discipleship and the portrayal of Jesus as the suffering servant. These two sections are clearly divided by Peter's confession in Mark 8:27-30. Here Peter reinforces Mark's opening line in Chapter One by basically repeating the first part of that verse: "You are the Christ". Then in Mark 8:31 Mark's Jesus tells them that the Messiah is not the kind of Messiah they are expecting. Rather, he is going to be the Messiah who suffers and dies. Yet, even though these two major themes are almost self-evident there are many other themes that are not as obvious.

### John the Baptist (1:2-11)

John the Baptist (JB) is found at or near the beginning of all four Gospels. Mark and Luke begin with a quote from Isaiah 40:3 referencing JB as "the voice of one crying in the wilderness". Matthew and John place the quote on the lips of JB himself. Mark's material about JB is much briefer than the other three Gospels. He simply tells us that he appeared in the desert, called people to repentance and baptized them in the Jordan River. Mark's John, like Matthew's and Luke's, predicts that there is one who is mightier than he who will baptize, not with water, but with the Holy Spirit. Mark describes JB as clothed with the garb of the prophet Elijah. Jesus refers to John as Elijah who has already come (Mark 9:1-13). Jesus submits to John's Baptism, which marks the beginning of his ministry. It is at that moment that Jesus is filled with the Holy Spirit when Mark says, "the heavens were torn open and the spirit, like a dove, descended upon him" (1:10).

Luke tells us that JB was a cousin of Jesus and the son of Zechariah, a priest. Herod Antipas executed John because he denounced Herod's immoral behavior. The Jewish historian, Josephus confirms this although he makes no mention of Matthew's elaborate account of John's head being brought to Herod's wife.

No one was closer to JB than Jesus. He was John's disciple and as such must have believed in and accepted John's message and his role as an eschatological prophet.[11] In the beginning, their message was essentially the same: "Repent for the Kingdom of God is at hand." But Jesus was different from JB. John was an ascetic, who fasted and took no strong drink. Jesus was extremely social and ate and drank often. John was judgmental and justice oriented. Jesus condemned judging others and was extraordinarily merciful.

Several scholars believe that JB was an Essene. Essenes were an ascetic group of Jews who were found in all the major cities of Israel. Some of them lived a monastic style of life in Qumran near the Dead Sea.[12] While there is no absolute proof that JB was an Essene he certainly embraced some of their ideas and life style and he also practiced his ministry very close to Qumran. There is a fair amount of evidence in the Gospels that the early Church used practices, which were quite similar to the Essenes, indicating that perhaps some of the disciples may have been Essenes.

## The Kingdom of God

Even a quick perusal of Mark leaves the reader almost breathless. There is a great sense of urgency in this Gospel. Over and over, he begins a new paragraph with the word "immediately". In fact, he uses it so often that modern translators replace it with other words such as: "then" or "soon after." This sense of urgency is likely because Mark feels that Jesus is going to return soon, certainly within a few years. He wants to make his readers aware of this so that they can properly prepare for his coming. As a result, the "Kingdom of God" is a major theme in Mark. Jesus, who is the Messiah

---

[11] Eschatology is the study of the end times, i.e. the end of the world, as we know it.

[12] The monastery at Qumran is the site of the Dead Sea Scrolls. These scrolls were discovered in 1947 and include all the Books of the Old Testament except to Book of Esther. There is also an extensive amount of other scrolls, which describe the community's lifestyle and beliefs.

and the Son of God, terms included in the opening verse of his Gospel, inaugurated this Kingdom. As I mentioned above, "Son of God" does not point to the divinity of Christ; rather it's a regal title. Since the Kingdom of God was inaugurated with the first coming of Jesus as Messiah, it would be fulfilled in his second coming when he will reign as King.

For the Jews there was only one King and that was God. Their earthly king represented God. It was God who led them into battle, God who conquered their enemies, God who set them free from oppression. Mark sees Jesus as the one chosen to represent God.

Messianic expectations were high during the early part of the first century **C.E.** Most expected the Messiah to be a great warrior king who would set them free from the oppression of the Romans and establish a universal kingdom to be ruled by the Messiah. The Kingdom of God in Mark certainly has the connotation of Jesus establishing a Kingdom. However, Jesus never says in Mark or any of the Gospels that he is going to lead them in battle against any nation of the world or set them free from the oppression of the Romans. He never admits that he is a king although Pilate recognizes him as such (15:9). The Kingdom for Jesus was a reign of justice and peace. It was emerging in and through him with tiny beginnings, like a mustard seed, which would grow to enormous proportions (5:30-32).

John's Jesus tells us that his kingdom is not of this world (18:36). Matthew's Jesus says that it is at hand (10:7). Luke says it's In our midst (17:21). For Mark, Jesus' miracles are a sign that the Kingdom is present in the world. Only God or his chosen one can do these wonders. Luke affirms this when messengers of John the Baptizer come and ask Jesus if he is the Messiah. Jesus responds by saying, "Tell John what you have seen and heard: the blind regain their sight, the lame walk, lepers are cleansed, the deaf hear . . ." (7:22).


## Miracles and Healings

One might call the Gospel of Mark "The Gospel of Jesus the Wonder Worker". I say this because a very large portion of this Gospel focuses on Jesus as a miracle worker. These miracles begin with the healing of Peter's mother-in-law (1:29-31) and end with the healing of the blind man Bartimaeus (10:46-52). The Gospel tells us Jesus cured many who were sick with various diseases and that he drove out many demons (1:34). So, Jesus was not only a healer but also an exorcist. Mark portrays Jesus in this way to show his compassion for the suffering and as proof that he was sent by God. All suffering and especially demonic possession was seen as evil and the result of sin. Only God or God's emissary would have the power to heal and cast out demons. Therefore, Jesus must be from God.

Some of the miracles in Mark also have symbolic meaning. When Simon's mother-in-law is healed she immediately begins to wait on those in the household. The early Christians were called to be servants and they served one another in their household churches. The healing of the blind man Bartimaeus is a story about faith. Often the word for "see" is synonymous with the word faith. Once Bartimaeus *sees*, he follows Jesus. Conversely, the blind man at Bethsaida "sees" gradually, indicating that some followers come to believe in Jesus slowly over a period of time.

The Gospel clearly states that healings and exorcisms are not only the result of the power within Jesus but also the faith of the believer. Notice in Nazareth (6:1-6), Jesus could not work any miracles there because of their lack of faith.


## The Messianic Secret

Often Jesus tells those who are healed and even those who have witnessed his miracles not to tell anyone about them (5:43, 7:26, and 7:36). When the demons recognize him he tells them to be still (Mk 1:34). Scholars have concocted elaborate explanations as to why Jesus was so secretive about his identity but I think that he simply wanted time to get his message out. The authorities were hostile to him from the very beginning, especially in Jerusalem. I think Jesus needed time and space. There are times when the report of his miracles caused such a stir that he "couldn't enter the town openly" (1:45). Then of course there was the danger of his messiah-ship being interpreted wrongly. Others who claimed to be a great warrior king had been quickly exterminated.[13] Jesus was not a political messiah although the term itself has political overtones. As we find out in Chapter 8, he is a suffering servant messiah, the kind that no one expected. Jesus was not going to lead the Jews in battle with the Romans; he didn't want that image

---

[13]    Judas the Galilean, a Jewish Zealot tried to lead a revolt against the Romans in 6 CE. He, along with his followers, was crucified.

to be a part of his Gospel message and that, in my opinion, is why he tried
to maintain some semblance of secrecy regarding his identity.

## Discipleship

Another theme, which is prevalent in Mark, is the meaning of discipleship
and its cost. Many of the members of the community in Rome were not good
disciples. They were weak and lacked faith in Jesus and they did not understand
his message. Mark points out that, even some of the Twelve were faithless and
didn't understand Jesus' message. Peter is a primary example here. Notice in
8:32 Peter rebukes Jesus and tries to dissuade him from following the path of
the suffering servant. Jesus responds with some of his sharpest words and even
calls Peter "Satan". The obvious message to the Christians in Rome is that even
the leader of the Twelve misunderstood the Gospel.

Then too there is Peter's denial. It is implicit that Jesus forgave him and
Peter went on to become one of the greatest apostles. Mark's message is that
if Peter misunderstood the message, if he could deny Christ in his darkest
hour, the Christian leaders in Rome shouldn't be too harsh with those who
failed to understand the Gospel and those who denied Jesus during the
persecution of Nero.

Some of the apostles, like James and John, wanted to rule with Jesus, to
sit at his right and left when he entered into his glorious reign (10:37). Surely
there were those in Rome who viewed the Kingdom of God as temporal
and sought to attain positions of power. (Unfortunately, little has changed!)
Mark's message is that, first of all, one must be willing to die for the sake of
the Kingdom and second, in death one will achieve his reward because the
Kingdom of Heaven is other-worldly and it's not about power.

Mark portrays the Twelve as being thickheaded and borderline stupid.
This is especially true of Peter. One wonders whether Peter really could have
been the source of this Gospel since he is portrayed in such a poor light.
Perhaps the editor did not have a favorable opinion of Peter or perhaps this
was Peter's way of self-deprecation, an expression of his deep sorrow for
betraying his Master.[14]

---

[14] It's no secret that Peter and Paul didn't get along. Paul's castigation of Peter
in Antioch over table fellowship with Gentiles was ill timed and, in my
opinion shameful. The fact that Paul was proud of it is even more shameful.

Over and over, we see Jesus trying to get his message across and over and over we see the Twelve not getting it. Unlike the other Gospels, especially Luke, even the women don't seem to understand. When the young man at the tomb announces Jesus' resurrection, instead of telling the disciples as in Matthew and Luke, they tell no one because they are afraid.

## Jesus and his Family

Mark 6:1-6 is one of the most striking accounts in this Gospel. Jesus returns to his hometown only to find that his own reject him. It is in this pericope (a brief vignette) that we are told that Jesus has four brothers and at least two sisters. "Is not this the carpenter, the son of Mary and brother of James and Joses and Judas and Simon and are not his sisters here with us?" (6:3). Protestants believe that these were children of Mary and Joseph; however, Roman Catholics and Orthodox Christians believe that Mary remained a virgin all her life, a teaching that became a doctrine in the Roman Catholic Church in 649 **CE** at a Lateran Council. As a result, the Catholic Church refutes this passage by saying that these are not children of Mary but rather they are cousins since the Hebrew and the Aramaic word for sister or brother can also mean cousin. While this is true, the Gospels were all written in Greek and the word used here is *adelphos* for brother and *adelphai* for sister. There is a word in Greek for cousin so if they were cousins why didn't the sacred authors use it? Note that Matthew, Mark and Luke all use *adelphos*. Paul, in his Epistles, always refers to James as the "Brother of the Lord". Again he uses the word *adelphos*.

The Orthodox Christians say that these brothers and sisters are children of Joseph by a former marriage. This teaching comes from a late second century "Gospel" known as the "Proto Gospel of James" which states that Joseph was a widower and was betrothed to Mary to care for her and she for him in his old age. The book is pseudo epigraphic meaning it was not written by James the Just, the leader of the Jerusalem Church and "brother"

---

See Galatians 3:11-14. Paul was highly educated and Peter was an illiterate fisherman, which would not have helped matters. If a disciple of Paul edited Mark's original Gospel he might have portrayed Peter as somewhat stupid. This, of course is a stretch but it would provide another reason why Peter is placed in such a poor light.

of Jesus but by someone long after James died. It is also very Greek and totally misrepresents first century Judaism and the Temple.

However, *adelphos* can be translated as stepbrother or half-brother so the Orthodox viewpoint can be reconciled with Scripture. Of course, if one accepts the virginal conception, all of Jesus siblings regardless of their origins would be half-brothers since Joseph was not the father of Jesus.

Still, even the stepbrother theory is not without problems. If Joseph had at least six children from a prior marriage, James, the eldest son, would have probably been a teenager when Jesus was born. If Jesus was born between 5 and 7 **B.C.E.**, the dates most scholars agree on, then James the Just was born somewhere around 19 **B.C.E.** This means he would have been in his fifties when he assumed the leadership of the Jerusalem Church and near 80 when he was martyred! The average life span in the first century Middle East was about 45. Eighty would have been very old and there's no indication in Acts or any other writings that James was anywhere near that age. Also, it seems more than a little irregular for an elderly man to marry a woman who is about the same age as his teenage son.

That said, there is no absolute way to prove this one way or another but I would have to agree that the scriptural evidence supports the Protestant view that these were children of Mary and Joseph. However, the evidence is not conclusive.

Another part of this pericope that needs some discussion is that we are told that not even his own kin or even those of his own house accepted him (6:4). John's Gospel states that Jesus' brothers did not believe in him (John 7:5). This seems strange, especially in light of the infancy narratives in Matthew and Luke. It's possible that the Evangelists want to contrast the importance of the new family of believers with Jesus' family to show that a follower of Christ must be willing to give up his family ties. This was very true among pagan converts. Once they had committed to the Christian life they no longer could eat with their families because of food restrictions: they couldn't go to the games in the arena—a family outing—and they couldn't offer sacrifice or give tithes to pagan gods—a family tradition. Christianity demanded a complete separation from one's old way of living. This is one of the reasons why Christians were so disliked by the Romans.

In Mark 3:31-35, Jesus' family asks for an audience with Jesus, "Your mother and your brothers are outside asking for you." Jesus replies, "'Who are my mother and brothers?' And looking around at those seated in the circle he says, 'Here are my mother and brothers. For, whoever does the will of God is my brother and mother.'" These seem like very strong words, and while it's certainly possible that, early in his ministry Jesus' relationship with his family may have been strained, it's likely that Matthew, Mark and Luke used all these examples to emphasize the total commitment to Christ required of his followers. After all, the Twelve Apostles left everything to follow him.

## The Calming of the Storm (4:35-41)

Perhaps the most telling story with regard to the persecution in Rome is the pericope about the calming of the storm at sea. While the story may have been based on an historical event I don't think the way it's portrayed is historical. I'd call it a parable in action, which is meant to teach a lesson to the survivors of Nero's persecution. If we look at the principle features of the story as allegorical we can understand the message. The boat was a well-known image of the Church in Rome. During the persecutions many Christians hid in the catacombs and a boat, which represented the Church, is often found drawn on the walls. Jesus is at the helm but he's asleep so it seems as though he's not paying attention to where the boat is headed. The storm represents evil and the waters the caldron of evil.[15] Note the power of this storm, which is symbolic of the power of Nero. Notice the words of the Apostles after they wake Jesus, "Lord don't you care if we perish?"

The Church in Rome had undergone the first great persecution in the history of the infant Church. Its members couldn't believe that Jesus would allow them to suffer so much. To them, it certainly looked as though the Church, i.e. the boat, was going to perish, i.e. sink. Why hadn't Jesus returned to save them? Was he asleep? Didn't he care about what happened to them?

In the story, Jesus rebukes the storm. The word "rebuke" indicates it's evil; one rebukes the devil not the wind. Then he says to the disciples, "Oh

---

[15]  The ancient peoples of the Middle East believed that evil spirits caused storms and natural disasters. Water, while it had salvific value, was also seen as the holder of evil and unclean spirits. Notice when Jesus sent the evil spirits of the possessed man into the pigs they ran off a cliff and were drown at sea (Mk 5:13). Baptism washes away sin and ritual baths removed ritual impurity. Both the sins and the impurities are in a sense made prisoners by the water. To be drowned at sea was considered to be a fate worse than dying by any other means.

you of little faith." Mark's Jesus is really saying these words to the disciples in Rome. He's reminding them that salvation comes from believing in Jesus. Their suffering is part of the consequences of being a disciple. Over and over in this Gospel, he tells his disciples that if they want to be true followers they must be willing to suffer for the sake of the Kingdom.


## The Little Apocalypse (13:1-36)

Chapter 13 of Mark has been called the *Little Apocalypse*. In it Jesus appears to be foretelling the destruction of Jerusalem and the end of a world. 13:1-3 is certainly about the destruction of Jerusalem. As I mentioned earlier, the Zealots wrested the city of Jerusalem away from the Romans. They turned the Temple into a fortress and awaited the coming of the Messiah who they believed would conquer the Romans and make Jerusalem the center of power where God would rule. The Romans, however, had other ideas. They sealed off the city and prevented supplies from reaching its inhabitants. This caused a great famine whereby many of the Jews starved to death. It was a horrifying experience. The contemporary Jewish historian Josephus tells a story of a woman who ate her own child! Disease took many to their graves. Eventually, in 70 **CE**, the Romans breached the wall of the city, killed the remaining inhabitants and destroyed the Temple.

Contrary to what we find in Matthew and Luke, Mark does not seem to be fully aware of the final outcome: hence, the dating of his Gospel before 70 **CE**. However, the handwriting is on the wall and 3:4-37 seems to combine the signs of the destruction of Jerusalem with the coming of Jesus at the end of time and it is difficult, at times, to differentiate the two. In this Chapter, Mark presents Jesus as an apocalyptic prophet. Remember, there is a sense of urgency in this Gospel as though everyone needs to get ready for an event that is to come in the future. That event for Mark's Jesus is the end of the world, as we know it. At that time, the hour which no one but the Father knows (13:32), the Son of Man will come on the clouds of heaven to gather the Elect (13:26-27).

13:9-13 gives us a brief history of some of the persecutions that had already taken place in the Church. Certainly, we know from Acts and Paul's letters that the apostles and others were dragged before both Jewish and Gentile leaders where they were interrogated, scourged and even stoned. Family members disowned their brothers and sisters, parents and children when threatened with bodily harm. Perhaps Mark is showing his readers that many of the things Jesus predicted have happened indicating that the time of judgment is near. Mark concludes with a mini parable warning the reader to be alert and keep watch because the end is near. Mark's Jesus even says, "this generation will not pass away until these things take place" (13:30).

One has to ask, "What things?" The destruction of Jerusalem certainly took place during the lifetime of some of the apostles' generation but Jesus still hadn't returned on the clouds of heaven to establish his kingdom. Yet, it seems as though Mark's is saying just that! How can we explain the discrepancy?

I believe that Mark, like the Twelve and others, including St Paul, believed early on that Jesus was going to return in their lifetime. Mark is writing his Gospel, either shortly before the deaths of Peter and Paul or shortly thereafter. Jerusalem was under siege and Nero had just finished persecuting the Christian community in Rome. There was famine in Jerusalem and the "abomination of Desolation" (13:14) appeared when the Zealots had desecrated the Temple. It must have seemed to Mark and his community that they were experiencing the end times. The lesson of the fig tree (13:28-31) seems to be saying that the tree is sprouting its leaves. This symbol indicates that the time is near. It's only a season away. Surely, Jesus would come soon to establish the Kingdom of God.

As we all know, that didn't happen. But Mark adds a qualifier. Jesus says that the Gospel must be preached to all nations (13:10). Surely, by 70 **CE** that had not occurred and it would not happen in the foreseeable future. Did a scribe who knew the outcome of these events in Rome and Jerusalem add this verse later? It's certainly possible.

The lesson to be learned here is that we can't take apocalyptic language literally. The main message, whether for Mark's audience or future generations, is that we cannot read these passages without knowing the context nor use them as a means to predict the future coming of the Messiah. One way to explain the discrepancies is that Mark is simply telling us we must not be misled by speculative predictions, yet we must always be watchful and alert.


## Jesus Christ Crucified (14:22-16:8)

The final lesson in this Gospel is that Jesus himself suffers and dies. Almost a third of Mark's Gospel is devoted to the passion and death of Jesus. Since it is such an essential part of the Gospel message I think it's important to go through it step-by-step.

The last straw for the leaders of the Jews seems to have been the cleansing of the temple (12:15-19). This event is mentioned in all four Gospels. John places it near the beginning of his Gospel (John 2:13-22) because for him the raising of Lazarus was the precipitating event. John also presents Jesus as replacing the Temple with his body which is represented by the body of Christ, i.e. the Church.

The activities which took placed in the Temple area were not secular. They were all connected with Temple worship. By casting out the money changers Jesus was directly challenging the authority of the Temple priests. These were the most powerful men in all of Israel. To challenge them would almost guarantee reprisal.

The Passion begins with the Last Supper (14:22-25).[16] Mark's supper was a Seder meal, a commemoration by the Jews of their escape from Egypt that recalls how the Angel of Death spared their ancestors because they sprinkled the blood of a lamb on the lintel of the door. While Mark makes no explicit reference to this, it's rather obvious that Jesus becomes a symbol of the sacrificed lamb. As the lamb's blood saved the people of Israel from physical death, the shedding of Jesus blood will save them and the world from spiritual death.

When Jesus passed the cup, said the blessing and then said, "This is my blood" the Twelve must have been more than a little disturbed. To eat or drink anything with blood in it is strictly forbidden by Jewish law. The word *Kosher* in part, means that there is absolutely no trace of blood in a meat product. In light of this the disciples would not have taken Jesus literally. It would be later, when the Church became separated from Judaism, that the notion of the "real presence" would be understood and accepted.[17] However, at this time, Jesus is focusing on his own sacrifice on the cross. Perhaps, even before the destruction of the Jerusalem Temple, his death would be seen as a replacement of Temple sacrifice. St Paul tells us that Jesus died once and for all for the forgiveness of sins (See Romans 6). The new covenant

---

[16]  Paul mentions the words of consecration in 1 Cor.11: 23-26, which is by far the earliest record, since Paul wrote this letter ten to fifteen years prior to Mark. However, Paul only refers to the Last Supper as the "Night before he died". He provides no other details.

[17]  John 6:52-66 addresses the problem of eating Jesus' flesh and drinking his blood in the Eucharist. Apparently his community was having difficulty accepting this and many left the community because of it.

would be sealed, not with the blood of animals but with Jesus' blood. Since everyone drank from the cup all would be one with him and become, as Paul often says, 'The Body of Christ." Unfortunately, they would all desert him, temporarily breaking the newly covenanted bond.

After this meal, Jesus and the disciples go to a place called Gethsemane. No other event brings out the humanity of Jesus more than Mark's version of what is known as "The Agony in the Garden" (Mark 14:32-42). Jesus is basically having a panic attack! He had no doubt seen many crucifixions and, like any human being, he doesn't want to die especially by crucifixion. Again his disciple's fail him. They fall asleep, leaving him alone to face his demons. His prayer in the garden, "not what I will but what you will" echoes the words of his mother in Luke 1:38, "May it be done unto me according to your word".

The betrayal of Judas is found in all four Gospels. The kiss makes the betrayal even worse. The early Christians greeted one another with a kiss. It was a sign of fellowship and love. Judas' kiss is a symbol of deception and treachery. However, we don't really know what was in Judas' heart. If he was a Zealot, a member of a political group that wanted to overthrow the Romans, perhaps he felt that turning Jesus in to the authorities would usher in the Kingdom of God and Jesus would be saved from crucifixion by an army of angels. The Zealot uprising in 66 **C.E.**, which led to the destruction of Jerusalem, was started with the firm belief that God would come to their aid.

The arrest of Jesus contains an interesting side story of a man in a white garment (14:51-52). We will see this man again at the tomb. The white garment may represent the baptismal robe that new converts wore when they came into the Church. The Greek word is *sindone*, which means "burial shroud". It symbolized that the newly baptized had been buried with Christ as they died to sin. The fact that he runs away, leaving the robe mirrors the betrayals of the baptized Christians in the Roman community. Leaving the robe means that he denied his baptism, i.e. his faith in Jesus.

Peter's denial (14:66-72) is found in all four Gospels so we can be certain that it happened. His words, "I do not know the man" are ironic. Throughout this Gospel, the disciples don't understand Jesus. In truth none of them really knew him.

Pontus Pilate was notorious for his cruelty. In fact, Roman documents indicate that Caesar removed Pilate from office, in part, because of his cruelty. Thousands of Jews were sentenced to death during his governorship.

The Gospels portray him differently. The fact that the Romans are portrayed in a positive light may have been because the Christian Church, especially in light of Nero's persecution, did not want to offend Rome and undergo another persecution.

The Persians developed crucifixion as a mode of execution. It was passed on to the Greeks and then to the Romans. The Romans used it as a deterrent to capital crimes. They refined it to the point where victims could hang on a cross for days before expiring. It was a public display of embarrassment and shame for the victim—they were naked—and a warning to all who might engage in anti-Roman activities.

Mark's picture of Jesus on the cross is one of utter aloneness. Judas betrays him, his disciples have all deserted him, Peter denies him and his own people reject him. Add to this the fury of all the people who are present, both Jews and Gentiles and we have a picture of one who is totally alone. No wonder he cries out "My Go, my God why have you abandoned me." (15:34) He is indeed like one of the animals that is slaughtered and sacrificed as a sin-offering in the Temple, which is exactly what Mark is trying to show. Jesus died for the sins of mankind

Surprisingly Jesus' death came quickly. Part of the reason was that he was scourged perhaps more than normal and he had to carry the crossbeam. Contrary to artistic portrayals of Jesus carrying the entire cross, the upright pillar was permanently placed in the ground so that it could be used over and over again plus it was far too heavy to carry. The victims died of asphyxiation. Usually, there was a footrest so that the victim could push himself up which would allow him to catch his breath. Jesus may not have had a footrest or he may not have wished to prolong his suffering allowing God's will to be done.[18]

The Book of Deuteronomy says, "Cursed is the man who is hung from a tree" (Deut 21:23). Perhaps that's why the leaders of the Jews adamantly wanted Jesus to be crucified. If he really were the Messiah, God would save him; if he died on the cross it would prove them right.

Imagine how dejected the disciples must have been; the one whom they had put all their trust in; the one who was to redeem Israel, was now a curse. They had left everything to follow him. Now he is dead, hung from a tree, and all seemed lost.

---

[18]   The Shroud of Turin, purported to be the burial cloth of Christ, shows hundreds of scourge marks indicating that this particular scourging was brutal. Tests made by various people indicate that asphyxiation is the cause of death. Apparently, the muscles in the upper chest tighten so much that the victim cannot catch his breath unless he pulls his body up with his arms or pushes it up with his feet. That is why breaking the legs hasten death.

Mark tells us that at the hour of his death, "the veil in the Temple was torn in two from *top* to bottom" (15:38). This curtain was thirty feet tall so it was God who tore it not man. The curtain separated the "Holy of Holies"; the inner sanctum of the Temple and the place only the High Priest could enter. The High Priest went into the Holy of Holies on the Day of Atonement to offer prayers for the forgiveness of Israel's sins. The symbolism is clear. Jesus, by virtue of his death has atoned for the sins of mankind once and for all. There is no longer any need for a high priest or a special feast. Mankind, no longer has to sacrifice animals for the forgiveness of sins. We are put right with God because the "Lamb of God" has taken away our sins by virtue of his death on the cross.

It's ironic that Joseph of Arimathea, a member of the Sanhedrin, the very body of people who condemned Jesus to death, provides him with a tomb. Crucified victims were normally thrown into a common grave. Mark uses the harsher word, "corpse" instead of "body" here to assure the reader Jesus is really dead. He says he was wrapped "in a piece of unused linen". Again, the word used here is *sindone*.[19]

Mark's Gospel specifically points out that the women came to the tomb after the Sabbath was over and after the sun had risen which literally means Sunday morning. Notice the young man is back. He is dressed in a white robe, the baptismal garment for the believer. He is not running away. There is no fear in him. He has donned the garment he left in the street the night of Jesus' arrest. Now he confidently announces that Jesus "has been raised . . . and he is going before you in Galilee"(16:6-7). Unlike the other Gospels, the women tell no one. Unlike the other Gospels there are no resurrection appearances in Mark. You might notice in your Bible other, additional endings. These were not part of the original manuscript. Scholars believe that the original ending could have been lost since it would have been at the end of the scroll and therefore worn away or torn off. However, since Mark's theme is discipleship and faith, the resurrection appearances may have been purposely omitted. You will notice in the other Gospels only people of faith could see the risen Jesus. Perhaps Mark's

---

[19]   As stated in a previous footnote the Shroud of Turin is such a cloth. The body would be laid on one end of the *sindone*, which was then draped over the front of the body. The Turin Shroud has two distinct images of a crucified man, which corresponds exactly to the narratives found in the Gospels. Numerous scientific tests support its authenticity. Carbon dating indicated that it was of 13th century origin. However, it has recently been proved that the samples used for these tests were flawed. Other tests prove that the Shroud is at least 1400 years old.

message to the people in Rome is that only people in the community who have faith can truly believe that Jesus was raised.

As I mentioned earlier, almost a third of Mark's Gospel is devoted to the passion and death of Jesus. This event became the heart of the Gospel message. It certainly was at the center of Paul's teaching. As he states in 1 Corinthians 15:12-19, "If Jesus didn't die and rise then we are the most pitiable of men." The final message for Mark is, "Yes, Jesus suffered and died. He became a curse who was hung from a tree, but God took the curse away by raising him from the dead." This was his message especially for the Roman Church. "Yes indeed, many of you have suffered and some have even died but your suffering was not in vain and, as Jesus was raised, so you also will be raised up on the last day which for Mark was coming soon."[20]

## WHO WAS/IS JESUS?

Each Gospel presents a different Jesus, however, the Jesus of Matthew, Mark and Luke is, in many ways, similar. Of course, one would expect this since Matthew and Luke used Mark as their primary source. Still, each of the Synoptics presents a Jesus who is unique to their story of him. Conversely, John presents a Jesus who is totally different from the Jesus of the Synoptic Gospels.

Before we discuss the Jesus of Mark and later, the Jesus of the other three Gospels, we need to understand how Jesus is understood today and how this came about.

---

[20] No only Mark but the early Church, from the time of its inception in Jerusalem, believed in the imminent coming of Christ. Paul certainly believed it as is evident in his earlier letters. How could these charismatic leaders so full of the Holy Spirit be so wrong? The obvious answer is they interpreted Jesus' words incorrectly. Perhaps this was because they, like us, so desperately wanted to see the end of the evil in the world that they read it into the message of Jesus. In reality, Jesus did return when he was raised from the dead. In a very real sense he returned when he sent the Holy Spirit, which Acts says, is the spirit of Jesus. Deep down, many of us would like God to put an end to evil and usher in a new world where, as Revelation 21:4 tells us, "There will be no more suffering and no more death." However, that's misplacing our responsibility as followers of Christ. The Kingdom of God is ushered in through the actions of those who dare to call themselves Christian not by God doing it for them.

I think we can say with a great degree of certainly that the first century Jerusalem Church basically viewed Jesus as a man who was empowered by God to perform miracles and other divine acts; who was chosen or anointed by God as the Messiah and because he was obedient to the will of God, even unto death, God raised him from the dead.

By saying this I mean that the disciples, including the Twelve, never thought Jesus was divine and Jesus, in the flesh, never told them he was divine. One might argue against these statements by saying that John's Jesus makes it very clear that he is divine and Jesus himself says that he is divine. While this appears to be the case, John's Gospel, as we shall see later, does not present the historical Jesus to us. That doesn't mean that John is wrong but again, as we shall see later, there is a very good explanation of how the Gospels can seemingly contradict each other and still be the inspired word of God.

The concept of a man being God or a god was an oxymoron for the Jews. It was an inconceivable notion and one, which diametrically opposed the teachings of Torah. This was one of the reasons they so hated the pagans. For one to even allude to the fact that a man or woman was divine was punishable by death. The Jews forbid images of any kind as a condemnation of pagan deities who were often represented by statues and amulets. Even their money did not contain any image since all images were considered to be "graven" i.e. idolatrous. The first century Jews were so against idolatry that even the worship of the one God via the use of another person or a picture was considered blasphemous. From this perspective, the Catholic devotion to Mary and the saints, for example, would have been totally unacceptable to the Jerusalem Church.

On the other hand, first century Jews believed divine power could be granted to beings other than God. For example, Lucifer, in the Book of Job, was given the power to wreak havoc on Job and his family. Moses was given the power and authority to work miracles and pass down the Law to the Jewish people. The fact that Jesus could work miracles and cast out demons was a sign, for the believer that he was from God and empowered by God.

However, the Gospels and Acts seem to indicate that this too could be construed as a form of blasphemy. In Mark 14: 61-62, the High Priest asks Jesus if he is the Messiah and Jesus responds, "I am; and you will see the Son of Man seated at the right hand of the Power and coming on the clouds of heaven." When the High Priest hears this, he declares that Jesus has blasphemed when, in fact, he has not. He has alluded to the figure in Daniel 7:13 who is cast as one who will judge the world. This is not a claim of divinity, only a claim that Jesus has been given the power to bring judgment upon the world in a way which I think is similar to Lucifer's judgment on Job.

Some say that Jesus' use of the Greek phrase *ego emi* (I Am), which is part of the divine name, "I Am Who Am" is blasphemous. I disagree with this because Jesus in the same sentence is careful to substitute the word "Power" for God indicating the typical Jewish sensitivity to avoid using the word "God". We see a similar case in Stephen's speech in Acts 7:56 when he says, "Behold, I see the Son of Man standing at the right hand of God." His Jewish listeners "cover their ears" a sign that Stephen has blasphemed and they stone him to death. If the Jews were this sensitive then there is no way Jesus could have told his disciples that he was God. They would have either left him or stoned him themselves!

So the notion that Jesus was divine evolved over a period of time. While I doubt that Paul, a Jew and a Pharisee could have conceived of a divine Jesus, his writings indicate that he certainly thought that Jesus was greater than angels. Like Stephen, he believed Jesus was given divine authority, to bring judgment upon the world. He refers to Jesus as *kuriou* which is the same word used in the Greek Septuagint for the name of God. However, *kuriou* was a title relegated to anyone who had authority so it does not mean that Paul thought Jesus was divine. Paul tells us in Romans that Jesus is the "new Adam". What he means by this is that the first Adam was not God but he was made in the image of God. When he sinned he no longer reflected God. Paul presents Jesus as the "New Adam" not God, but created in the image of God and, because he is sinless, he is the perfect or final Adam who truly projects the image of God.

John's Gospel certainly declares that Jesus is the same as God but this new understanding of Jesus was probably limited to just a few Churches in Asia Minor. The Ebionites, who were second century descendants of the Jerusalem Church, did not believe in the virginal conception or that Jesus was divine. They said God adopted Jesus at his baptism and his suffering and death was for the salvation of the Jews and that he would return to judge the world.

Other groups like the Docetists believed in two gods, the loving father of Jesus and an evil creator god who was the god of the Jews. Jesus was a divine being who only appeared to be human. They said he had no flesh and therefore, didn't really suffer and die on the cross. For them, all created things were evil so, in their minds, a human Jesus was an impossibility. Later in the third century, the followers of Arius taught that Jesus the son was not God as the Father was God and therefore was created by God.

Nestorius in the fifth century claimed that there were two persons in Christ, one divine and the other human in contrast to the Orthodox Church's teaching that in Christ there are two natures and only one divine person. It was the council of Nicaea that defined this doctrine in 325 **C.E.** Basically, it stated that Jesus Christ is "true God and true man" i.e. two natures, hypostatically united in the one divine person we call God. It went on to say that even though he is one integrated person there are no elements of his humanity missing, except of course sin.

Unfortunately, this definition is the result of the influence of Greek metaphysics, which defines the way things are outside the realm of history. In other words, things are as they are. They don't have to do anything to be all that they can be. With regard to Jesus, Luke tells us that he "advanced in wisdom and age and favor before God and men" (Lk 2:52). Hebrews 4:15 tells us that Jesus is like us in every way but sin. These statements indicate that perhaps the incarnation is a process. While Jesus may indeed be true God and true man he embraced his divinity as he grew in wisdom and grace with age. Karl Rahner states that the incarnation is a divine movement (process), which was fully employed only with the death and resurrection of Jesus.[21]

I have laid this groundwork for you to help you to understand that Jesus is certainly like us in every way but sin and yet is also God. His actions are human actions, which reflect God's actions because he is doing God's will and in this sense God is acting through him and in him. It also means that Jesus had to grow in his relationship with God as we do. He too had to trust, obey, have faith, pray and even experience the dark side of human existence. As he did this he became more and more Son as he embraced more and more of the divinity that was integrated in his personhood.

In no way am I saying or even implying that Jesus was not divine. I fully ascribe to the teachings of the Council of Nicaea. However, I want to focus on the humanity of Jesus because I think it's vital for our understanding of God. Stop for a minute to think of the vastness of the universe. Even the most intelligent human beings cannot even begin to understand its size and scope. Then to say that there is a God who is responsible for creating it and all that's in it means that God is even more incomprehensible. The

---

[21] Karl Rahner, a German Jesuit, was probably the most prominent and influential Catholic theologian of the Twentieth century. He died in 1984

only person who can make sense out of God is Jesus and because Jesus is a human being he is comprehensible to we who are also human.

Without Jesus I would be an agnostic. However, when I reflect on the human Jesus and read about him in the Gospels, I can come to know God. Why? Because, God has presented himself to me as a human being, and I can understand human beings, at least to some degree. Also, if Jesus wants me to follow him and lead the kind of life he led, be the kind of person he was, then he must be human. We cannot be God. We can't even be like God unless we have a concrete and identifiable example. Jesus as a human person provides that example.

Many people think that Jesus looks like a man but is really God inside or they think that he knew everything from the time he was a child or that he took on a perfect human condition. Some of these ideas are borderline heresies and certainly contradict Luke when he/she said that "Jesus grew in wisdom and favor before God" (2:52) or the Letter to the Hebrews statement that Jesus is like us in every way but sin (4:15). I find the fact that Jesus had to walk a journey of faith, like you and me, comforting because then I can readily identify with him and his life. I have an example to follow which is valid and in a sense attainable.

In spite of all this, Jesus is also divine, which means he had to have a unique relationship with his Father in Heaven. I think we can presume that he was especially gifted and/or that he had insights which were more unique than other human being. However, the New Testament reminds us several times that Jesus, i.e. God, chose not to be important or wealthy or unique but rather chose to be a servant; in other words a person who was not special. All of this, of course is a mystery, a mystery that we can never comprehend. Suffice to say that God loved us so much that he humbled himself to become a rather simple and unpretentious human being who preferred to serve rather than rule. This has to be the most extraordinary event in human history!

## MARK'S JESUS

Mark 1:1 opens his Gospel with the words, "This is the good news of Jesus Christ and the Son of God." Christ is the Greek word for Messiah. So it appears that Mark's goal is to prove Jesus is the long awaited "anointed one of God", the meaning of the word "Messiah", and that he is also the Son of God. Again, we must understand that neither of these titles indicates Jesus was divine. Nowhere in the Hebrew Scriptures or in Jewish tradition is the Messiah said to be a divine figure. Also, every Jewish male was referred to as a son of God and the King of the Jews was referred to as *the* Son of God. The title, "Son of God" indicates that Jesus is not only the Messiah but also that he is the King of the Jews. So this opening line in Mark's Gospel is saying Jesus is an apocalyptic deliverer who will free the Jews from oppression, in this case the oppression of sin, and eventually will establish a kingdom.

## A Human Being

Of all the four Gospels, Mark's Jesus is by far the most human. He is portrayed as a Jesus who struggled with his identity and questioned his disciples as to his true identity. Was he the Messiah, a prophet or simply a miracle worker and a teacher? I don't think Jesus was playing games with his disciples by asking them a question, about which he knew the answer. When he asks in 8:26, "Who do you say that I am?" I think he is seriously trying to understand who he is and his mission. He has an idea about who he is and God's will for him but he needs confirmation from his closest friends. When Peter confirms his suspicions only then is he convinced that he is the Messiah but now he's also certain that he is a Messiah who is going to suffer at the hands of the Jewish and Roman leaders.

Often, in Mark, Jesus spends time in a deserted place alone in prayer. While we do not know what he was praying for, we might surmise that he was asking God for direction regarding his ministry and an understanding of God's plan for him. In other words, nothing was absolutely clear. Unlike John's Jesus, Mark's Jesus certainly does not know everything. For example, he did not know what his disciples were talking about and had to ask them in 9:16, 33. In 14:33 he admits that he does not know the time or the place when the end of the world is going to happen.

Mark's Jesus is disappointed and saddened when his own townsfolk reject him and he is amazed by their lack of faith (6:1-6). Even more troubling was the fact that his mother and brothers thought he had lost his mind and came to take him home to put him away (3:21).

The humanness of Jesus is probably most obvious in the Garden of Gethsemane (14:33) where he literally has a panic attack. Mark tells us that Jesus is "*deeply* troubled and distressed" (italics mine) pleading with God to spare him from crucifixion. Matthew softens these words and Luke excludes them completely, even though he is using Mark's passion as his primary source. John doesn't even mention this garden agony. On the cross Jesus is so distraught that he cries out, "My God my God why have you forsaken me?" (15:34). Luke and John find these words so disturbing they omit them.

## The Son of Man

Mark's Jesus refers to himself as the Son of Man fourteen times. It's a mysterious title, *bar nasha*, in Hebrew which can simply mean a human being. God refers to Ezekiel as "son of man"(Ez 37:3). Perhaps Jesus is identifying himself as a prophet by using this term. However, I think Jesus uses it to conceal his identity and reveal it at the same time. Most likely it is a reference to the vision in Daniel 7, which describes "one like a Son of Man coming on the clouds" to judge the world. As I mentioned earlier, Jesus uses this apocalyptic terminology when he addresses the High Priest. Perhaps this is Jesus' way of saying that he is a man and at the same time revealing that he will be the heavenly being upon whom God has entrusted the authority to judge the world. It is an apocalyptic title that fits well into Mark's apocalyptic theme.

## The Son of God

As I mention above, the term "Son of God" is not a divine title. When applied by Mark to Jesus it means that he is the King who will usher in a new age, an apocalyptic age, marked by the end of the world, as we know it. Jesus will rule over this new age. For Mark, this rule will not just be over the Jews but the whole world. This is indicated by the Centurion's cry, "Truly this man was the Son of God" (15:39).

## The Miracle Worker and the Exorcist

Fr. Hodous, my college theology instructor, described Mark's Gospel as the "Gospel of Jesus the Wonderful". Throughout the Gospel, compared to Matthew and Luke, there is a limited amount of dialogue and a lot of miracles and exorcisms. Jesus cures lepers, makes the blind see and the deaf hear, and casts out demons, even legions of demons. Until Palm Sunday, no chapter is without a miracle. Jesus seems reluctant to work miracles yet he seems compelled to do them because he has compassion for those who are suffering. The conventional wisdom of the time believed that sickness and disease were the result of the afflicted one's personal sins or the sins of one's parents. By healing them Jesus is saying that he not only heals the body but the soul as well. Driving out demons means that he has power over evil, a power that can only come from God.

In spite of this, Jesus seems to want to keep his ministry of healing a secret since he often tells those who are cured not to tell anyone about what happened. Scholars call this the Messianic Secret and they differ widely regarding its interpretation. Personally, I think that Jesus is on the lam. Mark 1:14 begins with the words, "After John had been arrested, Jesus came to Galilee . . ." John's Gospel tells us that Jesus had an extended ministry in Judea before John's arrest. Jesus had very close ties to John so it might have been obvious to him that he too would be arrested. His movement in Galilee seems to support this. He spends a lot of time on the Western shore of the Sea of Galilee where he can easily cross over by boat to the Gentile territory of the Decapolis. In fact, he goes to the Decapolis and then to Tyre and Sidon in Syria. Peter's confession takes place in Caesarea Philippi, only a few miles from the Syrian border. Jesus is trying to stay under the radar so to speak.

Even though he's afraid of being arrested, Jesus continues to heal and exorcise demons because he has great compassion and also these are signs of who he is. When the followers of John the Baptist ask him if he is the Messiah he tells them, "Go back and tell John what you have seen and heard: the blind regain their sight, the lame walk, lepers are cleansed, the deaf hear, the dead are raised and the poor have the good news proclaimed to them" (Luke 7:22). Miracles and exorcisms are Jesus' way of showing compassion and also a subtle way of revealing himself as the Messiah, a Messiah who cleanses the afflicted of sin and who will suffer and die for the sins of the world.

## The Teacher

The people in the Gospel of Mark often call Jesus "Rabbi", which means teacher. Shortly after his baptism we find Jesus teaching in the synagogue and twenty times we find him teaching the crowds. That Jesus was a teacher is a given in all the Gospels. However, in Mark's Gospel he focuses mostly on teaching the disciples. In fact, in the second half of the Gospel, after Peter's confession, Jesus reveals that he must suffer and die only to them. He tells them that they too must suffer and perhaps even die for the sake of the Gospel. The sad part is that the disciples don't seem to understand his message. They fail to grasp the meaning of the transfiguration (9:5). They don't understand the purpose of his parables (4:13) or the meaning of the Kingdom (10:33-37). They can't believe his teaching about wealth (10:26) or the meaning of servant hood and its cost (10:35-45). Even the women don't understand as they say nothing about the resurrection because they are afraid (16:8).

So, in Mark, Jesus is a failure as a teacher. No one gets the message. This is not Jesus' fault but rather the fault of his listeners. They seem to be so blinded by the dream of a temporal kingdom that they can't understand Jesus' message which contradicts nearly all conventional wisdom. Even today, it seems most people don't really understand it.

## Conclusion

The Gospel of Mark presents a rather enigmatic Jesus. He is a person who has great power, divine power, but is powerless against the Romans and at the mercy of his captors. He's a miracle worker and an exorcist but in certain cases he's unable to work miracles. He seems strong and fearless but is terribly afraid of dying on the cross. He has absolute trust in God but questions God's fidelity on the cross. He is a great teacher who astounds the crowds but fails to get his message across to his closest friends. His identity, as presented by Mark, is as mysterious as the Messianic Secret. However, it is these incongruities that make Mark's Jesus so genuine. There's no fluff here. What we see is what we get and what we're getting is probably the closest we'll ever get to the historical Jesus.

## PERSONAL REFLECTION

I mentioned in the Introduction that the Bible can simply be read for personal reflection. One doesn't need a lot of background to do this and, quite frankly, I think when we open our hearts to the Holy Spirit we will find insights that will help us to understand God's plan for us. Consequently, after each Gospel I will provide my own personal insights on a theme found in a given Gospel. I hope this will help you to use the Scripture as a tool for personal reflection.

When I read Mark's Gospel the part that stands out most for me is Jesus' passion and death. Since it takes up one third of Mark's Gospel it must have been important to him as well.

Why did Jesus have to suffer? Surely, God could have come up with a better way. My response is that God did not send Jesus to suffer and die on a cross. Why would God do that? I certainly would never do this to my son or daughters and I am certainly no better than God!

God sent his Son into the world to do two things—to reveal God to the world and to save us from the consequences of sin. It was evil men who plotted against Jesus and put him to death.

God had every right to destroy those evil men; in fact God had every right to destroy the world. After all, we killed our God. Mankind committed the most heinous act possible. Yet, in spite of this, instead of destroying the world, God used this terrible crime to save the world. He turned Good Friday into Easter Sunday. The curse on the cross was turned into the savior of the world.

For me this is utterly amazing. It tells me how much God loves me and not just me but every single human person who has ever lived or will live. It also tells me that God wants to forgive far more than punish, to build up far more than tear down and to be merciful rather than just!

The passion of Jesus also gives me a little insight into the meaning of suffering. This, of course, is an age old problem. Why do people suffer? Even more so, why do good people suffer? Quite frankly, I don't know the answer to that question. However, God didn't spare Jesus from suffering; in fact, God let him suffer the terrible consequences of crucifixion. This tells me that suffering is a part of what it means to be human. Jesus was human and therefor he suffered. He suffered in spite of the fact that he led a perfect human life, in spite of the fact that he placed his complete trust in God, in spite of the fact that he always did God's will.

So I have to conclude that our suffering need not be in vain. If God can turn Good Friday into an Easter Sunday, then God can give meaning to our suffering. No one who was present at the crucifixion would have ever believed that good would come from it. When we suffer we can't imagine that good can come from it. Yet God sees the whole picture; we only see a tiny part of it. We only have an inkling of the master plan. God never causes us to suffer; however, God can give suffering meaning either in this life or in the next.

# Chapter Two

# THE GOSPEL OF LUKE

The Gospel of Luke is the most unique of the four Gospels because it is the first of two volumes. At one time, Luke and The Acts of the Apostles were a single composition. Sometime before the end of the second century they were divided into the two books we find in our bibles. A suitable conclusion was added with Luke 24:50-53 and the beginning of Acts was introduced with Acts 1:1-5. As a result, scholars now refer to the Gospel of Luke as Luke/Acts.

## WHO WROTE IT?

The author of Luke/Acts is identified as Luke, a disciple of Paul, by Iranaeus, the Bishop of Lyon, in the latter part of the second century.[22] The Muratorian Canon, a late second or early third century fragment, also identifies Luke as the author. Luke is a relatively unknown person. He's mentioned by Paul as a fellow worker in Phlm 1:24 and as "our beloved physician" in Col 4:14. It seems unlikely that the early Church Fathers would have given an unknown credit for this literary masterpiece unless he was probably the author.

Most believe that the Gospel was composed in Antioch although there are a few who designate Rome as the place of composition. Most of those

---

[22]    St Iranaeus (130 -200 CE) was a native of Smyrna near Ephesus. He became Bishop of Lyon in what is now France in 178 CE. He is most famous for his work, "Against Heresies" which is still intact.

who opt for Rome believe that the Gospel was composed during Paul's Roman imprisonment in about 62 **C.E.**

While there is little reason to reject Luke as the author, internal evidence in the Luke/Acts points to a person other than Luke and most importantly other than a man! I say this because the author of Luke seems unfamiliar with Paul's letters as well as Paul's life. Often, Acts contradicts details about Paul, which are mentioned in his letters. It seems to me, a companion of Paul would know these details.

Furthermore, the Gospel contains many unique stories about women, which are only found in Luke/Acts. These include: the annunciation by the angel Gabriel to Mary and Zechariah and the visitation of Mary with Elizabeth. Then there are the stories of Martha and Mary and Anna the Prophetess. Add to these the pericopes about the financial support of Joanna, Susanna and Mary Magdalene. Then there are the stories about the widow's son at Nain and the women who approached Jesus as he carried the cross.

When you read Luke you find that women are always portrayed in a positive light. With few exceptions men are portrayed in a negative way. The apostles are seen as slow to understand. They all desert Jesus and Peter denies him. They do not believe the woman's story that Jesus was raised from the dead. Contrary to Matthew, Joseph is a minor character in Luke's infancy narrative. Zechariah is struck dumb for questioning the angel while Mary questions him without consequences.

Ancient cultures, including the Greco-Roman world, deemed women to be second-class citizens. The continuum of life was basically about power and authority. Men were at the highest end of the continuum because they were the strongest. Women, being the weaker sex, were subject to men. Furthermore, a woman's testimony was not considered authoritative. In light of this, if a woman wrote Luke/Acts, she certainly wouldn't have gotten credit for it. Perhaps Luke was her scribe and, as such, was deemed by the Church to be the author.

As you read this Gospel, the Jesus you find therein is warm, compassionate, forgiving and sensitive, qualities which are more feminine than masculine. This is an unusual portrayal of a man, especially in ancient literature. Add to this the elements I mentioned above and a female author is plausible. My argument here is far from being conclusive. I only mention it as a point of interest.

## DATE OF COMPOSITION

Dating Luke/Acts is also a challenge. Acts describes the growth of the Church from the coming of the Holy Spirit on Pentecost to Paul's house arrest in Rome in about 60 or 61 **C.E.** Since Acts ends here it appears that Luke wrote it during Paul's Roman imprisonment. However, internal evidence in Luke/Acts indicates that the author used Mark as his/her primary source and is familiar with the details of the destruction of Jerusalem, which occurred in 70 **C.E.** Also, Luke 1:1 states, "Many have undertaken to compile a narrative of the events that have been fulfilled among us . . ." Who were these "many"? Mark was composed slightly before 70 **C.E.** Matthew and John were written much later. While there may have been an earlier version of Mark and perhaps a Hebrew sayings document these do not constitute many. The epistles cannot be included since they are not narratives. Even at the end of the first century we have no concrete evidence that there were any narratives about Jesus other than the four Gospels. So it's hard to believe that Luke/Acts was written in 62 **C.E.** Of course this begs the question as to why the author ended his masterpiece with Paul's Roman imprisonment.

Most scholars believe that Luke wrote this Gospel around 80 to 90 **C.E.** As I have stated above, some of this is based on the internal evidence that supports Luke's knowledge of the destruction of Jerusalem. Also, it is clear that Luke had a copy of Mark since Luke uses almost 60% of Mark. Often, he quotes Mark word for word. Where Mark's grammar or syntax is poor, Luke makes the appropriate corrections. Since the earliest probable date for Canonical Mark is 65 **C.E.**, Luke's Gospel could not have been written before that date. Mark's Gospel would also have needed time to circulate in the Christian communities and that's why scholars date Luke after about 80 **C.E.**

I personally think that Canonical Luke was written later than that. In fact, I would place its composition in the early part of the second century. I say this because the prologue's "many have undertaken . . ." implies that there were at least eight or nine written testimonies about Jesus that Luke was aware of. "Many" does not mean five or six and certainly not three or four. By the end of the first century the other three canonical Gospels were written. It's possible that, by the beginning of the second century, the Gospels of Thomas and Peter were also in circulation.[23] Scholars believe that other

---

[23] The Gospels of Thomas and Peter are early writings, which, while called Gospels, are really not of that genre. Peter only exists as a fragment and seems

writings may have been available by the early part of the second century. As I mentioned earlier, Mark may have written an earlier version of his Gospel in Aramaic. Most scholars now believe that a much simpler version of John existed as early as 70 **C.E.** Another document, posited by scholars, is called "Q" from the German word "quelle", which means source. This is believed to be a collection of the sayings of Jesus, which are found only in Luke and Matthew. Add all this together and you have "many Gospels or testimonies of Jesus but not until the second century.

# BACKGROUND

In spite of this evidence, Luke often seems primitive. I say this because there are many verses found in Luke, which are simpler than their parallels found in Matthew. A good example would be the Beatitudes and the Our Father, which are shorter than those from Matthew. Simpler usually means that the Evangelist is drawing from an earlier or older source. It seems to me that Luke is basically a compiler of sources which he/she has woven together into a single document. He/she may have remained very true to those sources, not wishing to change them or improve on them too much because he/she considered them to be written by important eyewitnesses.

Still, it's possible that there was an earlier form of Luke, which was edited in the early part of the second century. While it can't be proved that there was a proto-Luke/Acts, there may have been an early form of the Gospel without the infancy narratives and Luke's famous parables as well as other additions. Luke could have used Aramaic Mark and Q as his original sources and wrote the Gospel and Acts around 62 CE. An editor, perhaps the woman I mentioned above, added the infancy narratives and the other parts of Canonical Luke sometime during the first part of the second century.

I make these posits to show the reader that there are no foolproof explanations for the origins of the Gospels. We simply do not know for sure when they were written or who wrote them. I also want to point out that it's unrealistic to say

---

to focus on the crucifixion and death of Jesus. Thomas, which we have in its entirety, contains a group of 114 sayings of Jesus. Thomas is called a Gnostic writing because it engenders a philosophy stating that esoteric knowledge is required for salvation rather than belief in the suffering and death of Jesus. The early Church declared both books heretical.

that any of the Gospels, at least as we have them today, were written in one sitting. Common sense dictates a number of re-writes. Certainly, early Greek and Jewish scribes were extraordinarily gifted regarding their profession but anyone who has written even something as simple as a one-page reflection paper knows that it doesn't come out perfect on the first try. We shall see later that the early Church's understanding of Jesus changed considerably during the first century and so the Gospels needed to be changed accordingly. This is certainly most evident when we compare the other three Gospels to the Gospel of John.

I think it's important to understand that Gospel formation was a process and the Canonical Gospels took shape over a period of time, which may have included several edits along the way.

One aspect of Luke which really stands out is his/her eloquence. Luke is certainly a gifted writer and a wonderful storyteller. No writer in the New Testament is as articulate and fluent in Greek as Luke. In fact, he/she begins the Gospel using Classical Greek, probably to impress Theophilus, and then continues with common or koine Greek. Most likely Theophilus and his community were learned and certainly the quality of language used in this Gospel indicates that Luke was also quite learned.

Luke's stories and parables are masterpieces of presentation and drama. They are stories that speak of compassion and forgiveness. The words of Jesus resonate with the poor, the outcasts and the marginalized and at the same time severely indict the proud and the self-righteous. Without a doubt, Luke/Acts is a literary treasure and it is the most quoted of all the Gospels.

## HIGHLIGHTS AND THEMES

Luke addresses his/her introduction to Theophilus which means, "Lover of God". This person could be a Greco-Roman official or simply anyone who is a fellow Christian. Luke tells us his/her objective in this prologue: "I too have decided after investigating everything accurately anew, to write down an orderly sequence . . . so that you may realize the certainty of the teaching you received" (1:3). So, in essence, Luke is saying that he/she is going to set things right regarding the Gospel message and the growth of the early Church. Luke wants to present the whole story with Jesus initially proclaiming the Gospel to Israel and then his disciples proclaiming the Gospel to the world. This is symbolized by the Gospel's lowly beginnings in the remote Jewish town of Bethlehem and ending with a flourish as Paul freely proclaims the Gospel in Rome, the center of the Gentile world.

All this may be a clue as to why Acts ends so abruptly. "Setting the record straight" for Luke is to demonstrate that Christianity is an extension of Judaism. It is different from Judaism because it desires peace with all people, especially the Romans. Unlike the Jews, Christians have no intention of overthrowing Rome but their religion is rooted in Judaism and, as such, they should not be subjected to persecution.[24]

Even a rudimentary comparison of the Gospel with Acts shows that the growth of the Church parallels the ministry of Jesus. Luke/Acts does this to show the universality of the Gospel message and the shift of religious authority from Jerusalem to Rome.[25] A simple comparison is given below:

| *Jesus' Ministry in Luke* | *The Early Church in Acts* |
|---|---|
| Galilee/Jerusalem | Jerusalem |
| Forty days in the desert | Forty days before Ascension |
| Samaria | Samaria |
| The Decapolis | Asia Minor |
| Jesus anointed with Holy Spirit | Pentecost |
| Preached with power | Apostles preached with same power |
| Heals sick | Apostles heal the sick |
| Jesus' death | Stephen's death |
| Preach to all nations | Paul preaches in Rome |

None of this was done by accident. Luke divides salvation history into three parts: 1) the time of the promise, which through the infancy narrative and John the Baptizer, the prophecies are fulfilled and the Messiah has arrived, 2) the time of Jesus with his preaching, exorcisms, miracles, and the

---

[24]  Any religion, which did not have a long history, the Romans called a "mystery religion". As such, it was subject to persecution. After the destruction of Jerusalem, Christianity steadily moved away from its Jewish roots so that, by the second century, the Romans deemed it a separate religion.

[25]  This is another reason why I believe Canonical Luke was composed in the second century. In 62 C.E., Jerusalem was the center of the Church. In 75 C.E. it was Antioch, Syria. This means that, prior to the destruction of Jerusalem, Christian communities looked to Jerusalem for direction. After the destruction of Jerusalem, authority shifted to Antioch. It wasn't until the second century that Rome began to emerge as the authoritative center of Christendom.

ultimate fulfillment of his mission with his passion, death and resurrection and 3) the time of the Church in Acts where the mission continues through Peter and Paul and the Church's spread from Jerusalem to Rome.

## The Infancy Stories (1:5-2:40)

Perhaps the most unique part of Luke is his/her infancy narrative. Of the four Gospels only Luke and Matthew have stories about the birth of Jesus. If we compare Luke's narrative to Matthew's we find that they are quite different. Luke's has a lot more material compared to Matthew, especially with the stories of the birth of John the Baptist, the Visitation, the Annunciation and the events in the Jerusalem Temple. The table below details most of these differences:

| *Material Unique to Matthew* | *Material Unique to Luke* |
|---|---|
| The Magi | Elizabeth and Zachariah |
| The Star | Birth of John the Baptizer |
| Focus is on Joseph | Focus is on Mary |
| Mary and Joseph live in Bethlehem | Mary and Joseph live in Nazareth |
| Flight into Egypt | Gabriel and the Annunciations |
| Slaughter of the Innocence | Mary's Visit with Elizabeth |
| Return to Bethlehem after Herod dies | Anna and Simeon |
| Move to Nazareth | The Canticles of Anna, Simeon and Mary |
| | The Shepherds |
| | The Manger |
| | The Circumcision |
| | The Presentation in the Temple |
| | Return to Nazareth |

If we examine the texts carefully we find that some of the differences, regarding the story of the birth of Jesus, are irreconcilable. Luke tells us that Mary and Joseph lived in Nazareth and journeyed to Bethlehem because they had to register for a worldwide census, during the time when Quirinius was the Governor of Syria. Because they were unable to find a place to stay, Jesus was born behind an inn and laid in a feeding trough. After eight days, Jesus was circumcised and about a four weeks after that he was consecrated as their firstborn son in the Temple. Then they returned to Nazareth which means they were in Bethlehem/Jerusalem for only about six weeks.

Matthew, on the other hand, tells us that Mary and Joseph had a home in Bethlehem. Then, after the visit from the Magi, the Holy Family traveled to Egypt because Joseph had been warned in a dream that Herod was seeking to kill Jesus. They remained in Egypt until King Herod died which could have been a few years. After returning to Jerusalem, only then did they decide to move to Nazareth because they were afraid of Herod's son Archelaus.

Obviously, there are contradictions here but even without Matthew there are problems with Luke's account. Roman records indicate that Herod the Great died in 4 **B.C.E.** and the only census taken during Quirinius' governorship was about 6 **C.E.** Also, the census was not worldwide and women did not have to register for a Roman census. Add to this the fact that no Hebrew woman would have been asked to travel anywhere after her sixth month of pregnancy much less the 75 miles of rugged terrain from Nazareth to Bethlehem. Mary was in her ninth month or at least close to it. The usual procedure was to confine a woman to her home after the sixth month and have friends and relatives take care of household chores.

So what are we to make of these discrepancies? We'd have to conclude that, either one account is right and the other is wrong, or, historically speaking they're both wrong. If we had to choose, based on the erroneous dates in Luke and the traveling demands made on Mary, we would have to say that Matthew is likely more accurate than Luke. However, I think that neither account is historically accurate. Both were written, not as history but as theology.

Some might wonder whether these stories are really the inspired word of God. After all, if they're not historically accurate or true, how can they be inspired? Well, inspiration has a lot more to do with theology than history. The question we always need ask is, "What is God trying to say to us through the inspired writer?" Luke's infancy narratives are pregnant with meaning and he/she has presented the message with eloquence and beauty. These nativity stories have been remembered, not just for generations but for millennia.

So then, what do these stories tell us? Actually, Luke has interjected several themes into his stories. Zechariah's beautiful canticle tells us that John the Baptizer has come to bring the knowledge of salvation to the Jews and prepare them for the coming of the Messiah. Simeon's canticle reveals that Jesus will be a light, not just to the Jews but also to the nations. The census is said to be for the "whole world" which points to the universal salvation proclaimed by the Good News of Luke's Jesus.

Luke's use of shepherds, considered to be sinners and outcasts, combined with Mary and Joseph's lowly station in life plus the birth of Jesus in a stable, highlight the fact that the Gospel is for the poor and the marginalized.[26]

The Holy Spirit plays a very important role throughout Luke/Acts but it is especially provocative here. Notice that John is filled with the Holy Spirit from birth, Elizabeth is filled with the Holy Spirit during Mary's visit, and John and Jesus are conceived through the power of the Holy Spirit. Simeon, Mary and Zechariah are filled with the Holy Spirit when they recite their canticles. Anna is a prophetess, a title that means she too is filled with the Holy Spirit.

The power of prayer is also an important theme here. All the canticles are prayers and notice that the text tells us Zachariah's prayer was heard (Luke 1:13) and of course answered.

Another important topic in Luke's infancy narrative is the portrayal of Jesus as being superior to John the Baptizer.[27] Still, Luke makes sure that the reader understands that John is indeed a great prophet. In fact, in Luke 7:28, Jesus says that no one born of a woman is greater than John the Baptizer.

Notice the similarities between the stories of the birth of John the Baptizer and of Jesus. In both narratives, the parents are named and both are the result of a miraculous conception. Zechariah's canticle is contrasted with Mary's. John grew and became strong in spirit. Jesus grew in wisdom and favor. However, while John will be "great in the sight of the Lord" and will "turn many of the children of Israel to the Lord" (1:15-16 ) Jesus "will be called the Son of the Most High" and "will rule over the house of Jacob forever and of his kingdom there will be no end" (1:32-33).

---

[26]   At the end of a Jewish woman's purification (the time required to be cleansed from the issue of blood from the birth of her child) the normal offering in the Temple was a lamb. The offering by Mary and Joseph of two turtledoves indicates that they were quite poor. However, Luke may have used this as a theological device to foster his theme. Joseph was a tradesman and owned a house indicating that the family was far from poverty stricken.

[27]   Apparently, the Baptist's movement continued through the end of the first century. In Acts 18:25 we are told that Apollo only knew the baptism of John. Some even believed that John the Baptizer was the Messiah not Jesus. After all, it was John who baptized Jesus not the other way around. Both John and Luke attempt to clear the air by making sure that John the Baptizer is presented as being inferior to Jesus.

When we have verses so packed with meaning it really doesn't matter whether the stories are historical. God is saying so many things about the mission of the Baptist and Jesus that we need to bypass the historical aspects to get to the heart of what's really being said here.

These stories also act as a sort of preface to Luke/Acts. The themes are a premonition of what Luke is going to say in the rest of his/her masterpiece. Over and over again, the universality of the Gospel will be proclaimed especially in Acts. The role of the Holy Spirit continues to be prominent, not only in the Gospel but also in Acts. In fact, Luke/Acts has been called the Gospel of the Holy Spirit.

## The Poor and the Marginalized

No other Gospel focuses on the care and concern for the poor and the marginalized more than Luke. As we have seen, the shepherds are the first to hear of the birth of Christ. Shepherds, who were deemed unclean and outcasts by the priests and rabbis, hear this Good News directly from the angels in heaven. Jesus is portrayed as being a friend of publicans and sinners[28] (7:34). Only Luke has the story of Zaccheus, the wealthy tax collector (19:1-10). It's also interesting to note that some manuscripts of Luke contain the story of the woman caught in the act of adultery. This story was added to the Gospel of John in the second century and was therefore, not a part of the original. Perhaps it originally came from Luke.

The Zaccheus story gets to the heart of Jesus' relationship with sinners. Jesus never says that it's all right to be a sinner. What he's saying here is that it's all right to be tax collector as long as you're not a sinner. Notice that Zaccheus' meeting with Jesus leads to his conversion. In fact, it is such a great turn-around that he does far more than what is expected. He promises to give half his income to the poor; Jewish Law required only a tenth. He promises to repay those he cheated four-fold; the Law of Moses only required that one pay the money back with interest. Jesus words at the end of the

---

[28] These are terms used for those known as public sinners, which primarily meant prostitutes and tax collectors. Tax collectors were seen as traitors because they collected tax for the Romans. They also extorted money for themselves. Prostitution was a public crime because it destroyed the family unit, which was of utmost importance for the Jews.

story reaffirms his message in Luke, "For the Son of Man has come to seek and to save what was lost" (19:10).


## Jesus' Sermons in Luke

Jesus' "sermons" in Luke, which scholars believe are from Q, parallels Matthew's Sermon on the Mount (Matt. 5-7). Parts of Q are found in what Scholars call "The Sermon on the Plain" (Luke 6:30-49) and other sayings scattered throughout the Gospel. Matthew compartmentalizes these sayings into one great sermon whereas Luke more or less randomly places them throughout his/her Gospel. As I mentioned earlier, this material is believed to be part of an oral or written tradition, which circulated in various Christian communities. Luke's Q material is more terse than Matthew's indicating that perhaps it's either taken from an earlier source or Matthew expanded the material to fit his agenda.

An excellent example is the "Our Father". Compare Matt 6:9-15 to Luke 11:2-4. Notice the simple address, "Father" in Luke followed by a simple word of praise. I believe Luke is probably an older version, which is closer to the original mainly because it is so much simpler and shorter—in Greek, 38 words versus 58 in Matthew.

Luke's Beatitudes are also quite different from Matthew's. There are only four versus Matthew's nine. Luke's, as always, are shorter and simpler. It seems apparent that, again Luke is older and closer to the original. For example, Luke says, "Blessed (*makarioi* in Greek) are the poor", Matthew says, "Blessed are the poor in spirit". Luke says, "Blessed are you who hunger now", Matthew says, "Blessed are you who hunger and thirst for righteousness". Luke is plain and simple. Matthew qualifies his statements. I'm sure that if Luke knew of the other five Beatitudes in Matthew he would have used most of them if not all.

Luke also differs from Matthew by adding a collection of woes. As I mentioned above, Luke champions the poor and the outcasts and he often contrasts them with the rich highlighting the poor in a positive way and the rich in a negative way. I don't think Jesus condemned wealth. We must remember he often dined with the wealthy; Zacchaeus is a case in point. However, wealth leads to greed and waste often at the expense of the poor. For Jesus, the wealthy have an opportunity to rid the world of poverty and oppression. That is the way they find salvation, again as Zacchaeus did.

Luke is not saying that the poor, the hungry and those who weep are fortunate (another translation for the Greek word *makarioi*) strictly because of these traits. Rather, he is saying that, because they belong to the community of believers, those who follow Christ, they will no longer be hungry, or poor or sad. Acts 2:44-45 tells us that the early Christians shared everything in common so that no one went without. Therefore, rich or poor, everyone had the necessities of life and they were all filled with the joy of the Holy Spirit. They were the ideal community, the Kingdom of Heaven on earth, a foreshadowing of what was to come. For Luke it was the poor and the outcast who accepted the Kingdom. Most of the wealthy rejected it.[29] As a result it was "woe to them"!

## Luke's Parables

A parable is a metaphor in story form. Its main purpose in the Gospels is to challenge the listeners to reflect on their lives especially in terms of how their behavior conforms to the will of God. They are different from allegories. Allegories have subjective meaning wherein the characters or things represent someone or something else. For example, when Jesus says, "I am the vine and you are the branches" we know that he is not really a grape vine and we are not the shoots that spring from that vine. Contrast this with "The Kingdom of Heaven is like a mustard seed, that when sown in the ground is the smallest of all the seeds on earth." It's easy to see the difference. Believers know that the Kingdom of Heaven is like a seed. They do not have to guess what the seed represents.

---

[29]   Since most of the Jews of Jesus' day did not believe in an afterlife, and that God was just, people were rewarded or punished by God in this life. The rewards were temporal as were punishments. Therefore, wealth and social status were viewed as the result of righteousness. God had rewarded them because they were good. If they were poor or were afflicted with a disease like leprosy or blindness it must be because they were sinners or they came from a family of sinners. Obviously, such an attitude provided an air of superiority for the wealthy and the seeds of oppression. Jesus condemned this mind-set saying that temporal wealth or status was irrelevant in God's eyes. Sincerity of heart is what mattered. Accepting the message of Jesus was the key to divine acceptance. Many, who were wealthy and/ or important, found this teaching unacceptable.

Certainly, Jesus loved to tell stories and it seems apparent that he was an outstanding storyteller. I believe, in their original form, his stories were simple and to the point. He used everyday images, images that were familiar to his audience, things that they could easily relate to; things in the fields, in their houses and in their cities.

Obviously, the parables were initially directed to his fellow Israelites. The Evangelists directed them to the Greeks and Romans; today they speak to us. However, in the process of changing to a different audience, the Evangelists allegorized the parables so that they could be used as teaching tool.

Originally Jesus' parables were simple and very short. The average person would not fully get the connection. Only the true believer would understand them. This is why Jesus often followed a parable with the words, "Whoever has ears hear." To have ears was to have faith, which led to understanding.

## The Rich Fool (12:16-21)

An example is the parable of the rich fool. It is a parable that is unique to Luke but it is also found in the apocryphal Gospel of Thomas. The Gospel of Thomas is a second century collection of the sayings of Jesus. Scholars believe that while it is not as old as the four Gospels it draws from some traditions that may be older than the four Gospels. If we compare the parable of the rich fool in Luke to Thomas we can see how much simpler Thomas is and perhaps have a sense of the parable as Jesus himself told it.

"There was a rich man whose land produced a bountiful harvest. He asked himself, 'What shall I do, for I do not have space to store my harvest?' And he said, 'This is what I shall do: I shall tear down my barns and build larger ones. There I shall store my grain and other goods and I shall say to myself, "Now as for you, you have so many good things stored up for many years; rest, eat, drink and be merry!"' But God said to him, 'You fool, this night your life shall be demanded of you; and the things you have prepared, to whom will they belong?' Thus it will be for the one who stores up treasure for himself but is not rich in the matters of God" (Luke 12:16-21).

"There was a rich man who had a great deal of money. He said, 'I shall invest my money so that I may sow, plant and fill my storehouses with produce, that I may lack nothing.' These were the things he was thinking in his heart, but that very night he died" (Thomas, Logia 63).

Notice how much simpler Thomas' version is. There is no summary as in Luke 12:21. A lot of the details are missing. It's up to the listener to fill in the details and understand the message. I believe that Jesus spoke in this way. He kept it simple which made it much more challenging for the listener who really needed the gift of faith to understand it.

The Evangelists, writing forty to sixty years after Jesus died, felt they needed to provide insights to help the reader understand. Since allegory was very common among the Greeks, and since the Evangelists were either Greeks themselves or influenced by Greek culture, they allegorized Jesus' parables, which made them a powerful teaching tool for the Gentiles. Luke was, without a doubt a master at this. His/her stories of the "Good Samaritan", "The Rich Fool", "The Prodigal Son", "The Dishonest Steward", "The Rich Man and Lazarus" and "The Persistent Widow" are unique to Luke and some of them are literary jewels.

## The Good Samaritan (10:29-37)

The parable of the good Samaritan is one of the most well known parables, so much so that the phrase "good Samaritan" has become a cliché in the western world. The story is set up by the dialogue between Jesus and a "scholar of the Law" who asked him what must be done to inherit eternal life (10:25-28). When Jesus asks him what is written in the Law the scholar responds by repeating the great commandment about loving God and loving neighbor. The scholar challenges Jesus by asking him, "And who is my neighbor?" (10:29). Jesus responds with the parable of the Good Samaritan.

Some assumptions have to be made to get the full impact of this narrative. We have to presume that the victim is a Jew. We also need to presume that the priest and the Levite are on their way to Jerusalem to offer sacrifice in the Temple. Neither of these presumptions are a stretch of the imagination especially the latter since we are told that the priest and the Levite passed the victim on the opposite side of the road indicating that they were going to Jerusalem not to Jericho.

It then makes sense as to why they did not stop. Priests and Levites (a Levite was basically a second class priest) were allowed to offer sacrifice in the Temple once a year. It was a great honor, one they greatly looked forward to. If either were to stop they would probably get blood on their hands as they bound up his wounds or perhaps the man was dead. Both would make them ritually impure and they would miss their turn to offer sacrifice. This, of course, reflects Jesus' teaching that mercy is always more important than ritual or obedience to the Law.

Samaritans were hated by Jews and quite frankly the reverse was also true. Having the Samaritan not only help his enemy but go to great lengths to care for him enforces Jesus' teaching to love even your enemy (Luke 6:27, Matt. 5:43). Luke's Jesus ends the parable by having the scholar answer his own question, "Who is my neighbor?" "The one who treated him with mercy" (10:37).

In other words, it does not matter whether a person is a friend or an enemy, one who is loved or hated. The true disciple of Christ is merciful to all who cross his path.


## *The Prodigal Son* (15: 11-32)

I believe it was Ernest Hemmingway who said the story of the prodigal son was the greatest short story ever written.

"The Prodigal Son" is an example of pure allegory, such that if you do not know who the characters symbolize you will not understand the story. Luke helps us by preceding it with the "Parable of the Lost Sheep" (15:1-8) and the "Parable of the Lost Coin" (15:8-10). Both these parables have the same theme: " . . . there will be rejoicing among the angels in heaven over one sinner who repents" (15:10). "The Prodigal Son" says the same thing but in a different way, "We must celebrate because this son of mine was dead and has come back to life. He was lost but has been found" (15:24).

Once the groundwork is set, the allegorical symbols are clear. The younger son is you and I when we stray from our social, cultural and religious norms. The elder son is the righteous person who always obeys the letter of the law. In the original setting he would be a Pharisee; in a modern setting it would be righteous Christian who believes that obedience to the laws of the Church take precedence over mercy and compassion.

The father, of course, is God who is presented in a way that would have been totally foreign to the minds of both the Jews and the Greeks. I say this because the younger son pays his father the highest insult imaginable. His desire for an instantaneous share of the estate is essentially saying that he wishes his father were dead. It shows a complete disregard for the authority of his father and his family. He's a greedy little brat who needs to be severely disciplined which in the first century Jewish culture meant that he needed to be beaten with a stick and exiled from the family. Every Jewish father would have reacted in this way.

However, the father in this story is different from every other father. Luke simply says, "So the Father divided the property between them" (15:12), i.e. he and his older brother. The boy goes off, and as expected, squanders all his money. He realizes his mistake and returns to his father with a confession of repentance on his lips. Surprisingly, the father hasn't forgotten him. The normal father of that day would have written him off, demanded that the rest of the family forget that he had ever been born. Yet, this father restores him to his original status. The ring has the family seal, the robe means he is a son again and the sandals means that he is not to be relegated to the status of a slave. Everything is as though he never left. Why has the father done this? "Because this son of mine was dead and has come back to life again. He was lost and has been found" (15:24).

However, the parable doesn't end here. Actually, there are two parables: the first is about the younger son; the second is about the older son. When the elder son finds out that the younger son has not only come home but also that the father has returned him to his original status in the family he is livid. He refuses to go into the house to attend the welcome home party. As the father ran out to his younger son when he saw him on the horizon, he comes out to the elder son pleading with him to come in and join the celebration. But the elder boy will have none of it. To him the whole episode is unjust and unfair. He even refuses to call the younger son his brother (15:30). The father tells him that everything he has belongs to him and that they must celebrate because "your brother was dead and has come back to life . . ." But the elder son is obstinate. He refuses the father's invitation to be merciful and forgiving, which, according to Jesus' words in the Sermon on the Mount cuts him off from God's mercy (Matt. 6:15).

This amazing parable is an incredible testimony of God's love for us. Luke's Jesus tells us that God isn't nearly as concerned about rules and justice as He is about mercy and compassion. In fact, for Luke's Jesus, mercy and compassion always takes precedence over law. Notice in the story that the elder son, i.e. the righteous Pharisee, never really lost anything except his brother. He still gets half the inheritance; in fact the father says, "*Everything*

I have is yours." (Italics mine). He was upset only because he wanted to see his brother punished. He wanted to be there when his brother had to pay the piper so to speak. He was denied that and he was more than a little upset.

Often, in the Gospels, Jesus talks about the penalty for judging others. The way we judge will be the measure God will use to judge us. The way we forgive others will determine God's forgiveness (See Matt. 7:1-5). In the "Our Father" we've said thousands of times, "Forgive us our trespasses as we forgive those who trespass against us." Based on what Jesus has told us in the Gospels, those like the elder son will be denied salvation because they are heartless. Those who, like the younger son, are truly sorry for their sins will become citizens of the Kingdom of God.

## THE LAST SUPPER AND THE PASSION (22:14-23:56)

Unlike Matthew who closely follows Mark, Luke has either simplified Mark a great deal regarding the Last Supper and the Passion narratives or he is drawing from a different tradition. I believe it's the latter since he/she also adds material that is not found in either Matthew or Mark.

Some of the additions include: Jesus' earnest desire to eat the Passover supper with them (22:15-20), Jesus' promise to pray for Peter regarding his denial (22:31-34), the sending of an angel to comfort Jesus in the garden (22:43-44), Pilate sending Jesus to Herod (23:6-16) and the story of the good criminal (23:39-43).

Many of these additions demonstrate the compassion of Jesus, a theme that is prominent throughout Luke's Gospel. The "Good Thief" narrative stands out for a number of reasons. Notice that the man admits he's guilty of a crime but he never says he's sorry for his sins. He simply asks Jesus to remember him when he enters his kingdom (24:42). Jesus rewards him with eternal life which will be given immediately following his death. He's allowed to pass *GO*, collect his money and go straight to heaven! There's no punishment due to sin, no purgatory and no waiting. The key for Luke is that the man recognizes Jesus as the Messiah and so in this sense he becomes a Christian. The compassionate Jesus of Luke responds with the gift of eternal life, the gift which awaits every believer. This also contradicts the first century Jewish belief that the believer must wait until the Last Judgment before entering Paradise. Early on, this was also a belief of Jesus disciples (See John 11:24).

Some of the verses Luke omits include: the death of Judas[30] (Matt 27:3-10), the desire of Pilate to release Barabbas (Matt 27:15-18, Mk. 15:15-10), the omission of "My God my God why have you forsaken me" (Matt 27:46, Mk. 15:34) and Pilate's surprise that Jesus died so quickly (Mk. 15:44) to name a few.

Another curious difference is found in Luke's description of the Last Supper. According to Luke Jesus offers the cup before offering the bread. This is also found in the Didache which also uses a very different formula[31] This cup would be the first cup offered to everyone at the Seder meal over which each person would say a blessing. The NAB adds a verse to eliminate any confusion: "And likewise the cup after they had eaten, saying, "This cup is the new covenant in my blood which will be shed for you" (22:20). This verse is found in some manuscripts but not the oldest ones so it is omitted in the RSV.

In a sense Luke invites the reader to accompany Jesus on the road to Calvary. We can recognize ourselves in Peter's denial, carry his cross with Simon and commit our spirit to God when we take our last breath. There is a sense of comfort and peace here that is not found in the other Gospels

## LUKE'S RESURRECTION STORIES (24:1-52)

Unlike Mark, Luke narrates a few resurrection appearances. Luke is unique among the Gospels because all of the appearances of Jesus, including the Ascension, occur on the same day, Easter Sunday. Notice in 24:1 he starts with, "On the first day of the week . . ." In vs. 13 he says, "On that

---

[30] Luke mentions the death of Judas in Acts 2:17-20) however, he describes Judas as falling to his death rather than hanging himself as described by Matthew.

[31] Didache 9:1-4 says, "As for thanksgiving (Eucharist) give thanks this way. First, regarding the cup. 'We thank you, our Father for the holy vine of David your servant, which you made known to us through Jesus your servant. To you be glory forever.' Then with regard to the Bread: 'We thank you our Father for the life and knowledge which you made known to us through your servant Jesus. As this [bread] lay scattered upon the mountains and became one when it had been gathered, so may your church be gathered into your kingdom from the ends of the earth. For glory and power are yours through Jesus Christ forever and ever.'"

very day . . ." After the two on the road to Emmaus go back to the disciples "on that very day", Jesus appears to them, (24:36) and then leads them out to Bethany where he ascends into heaven (24:51). This is a contradiction of Acts wherein Luke tells us in Acts 1:3 that Jesus, "presented himself alive to them by many proofs after he had suffered, appearing to them for forty days . . ."

Obviously, Luke was well aware of the contradiction so, like the infancy narrative, he/she must have had something other than pure history in mind. For Luke, the resurrection inaugurated the "Day of The Lord" the moment in time when the old age, i.e. the Old Covenant, gives way to the new and everlasting covenant wherein everyone who believes in Jesus is put right with God. The early Christian community, those who followed the way of Jesus, called this day "The Lord's Day", to differentiate it from the Jewish Sabbath. It was the day on which they gathered to celebrate "The Breaking of the Bread", their name for the Eucharistic meal. This meal not only recalled the suffering and death of Jesus but also prefigured the Messianic Banquet; that great meal foretold by the prophets and also celebrated by the Essenes, wherein the elect would sit at God's table in heaven. So, this part of the Gospel is Luke's way of inaugurating "The Lord's Day".

In Acts, Luke is using the figurative number 40 to again separate the old age from the new age. The number 40 represents a generation. The passing of a generation marks the end of the old way of doing things and ushers in the ways of the next generation. For instance, the Jews wandered in the desert for forty years before they entered into the Promised Land. The people who went into Palestine were not the same people who were at Sinai. They were a new generation. The Jesus who came out of the desert after forty days was not the same Jesus who went into the desert. He was transformed from a recluse into a preacher, teacher and healer. So too in Acts, the 40 days marks the end of an age. Jesus will no longer be present to his followers in the flesh. They will not see him that way on earth again. But this ending marks a new beginning, the age of the Holy Spirit; "You will receive power when the Holy Spirit comes upon you" (Acts 1:8). The power of the Holy Spirit is a thread which has been woven into Luke's testimony since the Gospel's humble beginnings in Bethlehem. After the Ascension, the Holy Spirit will become the principle character in Acts, replacing Jesus in the flesh with the spirit of Jesus.

## The Road to Emmaus (24:13-35)

Like the "Prodigal Son", the story of the journey on the road to Emmaus is Luke at his/her best. It's really a parable in action wherein Luke has taken an historical tradition and stylized it to read like his/her parables. One of the two is identified as a man named Cleopas. John 19:25 mentions a woman at the foot of the cross as "Mary the wife of Cleopas". Traditionally, Cleopas is believed to be the brother of Joseph, the paternal father of Jesus. So, it's likely that the two people on the journey are husband and wife. They appear to be going to their home in Emmaus. I say this because they invite Jesus into a house where they are going to stay and they prepare a meal for him. There appears to be no one else in this house so it is not an inn.

Why are they going home? We are told that they are "downcast". In other words, not only are they grief-stricken because they've lost their nephew but also they are totally dejected because the "one they had hoped would redeem Israel" (24:21) was dead. Not only was he dead, he was hung from a tree and therefore could not be the Messiah. Remember, according to Jewish Law, anyone hung from a tree was God's curse. So, we can assume that they now realized that all their hopes and dreams were shattered. They had given two or three years of their lives to Jesus and it was over. There was nothing else for them to do but go back to their old way of life.

Then Jesus appears to them. But the text says, "They were prevented from recognizing him." What prevented them from realizing that it was Jesus? In part, it was their lack of faith. The Gospels make it clear that only people of faith can recognize the risen Jesus. They lost their faith when Jesus died.

When Jesus asks them why they are so downcast, Cleopas responds with a creedal statement. Notice how his words summarize the Gospel message. Compare his words to Acts 2:22-24, the beginning of Peter's sermon on Pentecost. These statements were the heart of the early Church's testimony about Jesus. Cleopas does it unwittingly but the message is clear.

Then Jesus explains the Scriptures to them to show them how all this was foretold in the Hebrew Scriptures. The early Church used Old Testament texts to prove that Jesus was who he said he was. Surely, the leaders of the Jews would have demanded such proof. This section of the story tells us that the risen Jesus, through the power of the Holy Spirit, guided the Church and pointed them to the appropriate texts, which explained and foretold his mission, especially his suffering and death. Their response, "Don't you remember how our hearts burned within us when he explained the Scripture to us?" is an indication that the disciples' rereading of the Old Testament in light of the Jesus Event was inspired and prophetic.

When they arrived at their home, Jesus gives the impression that he is continuing on but they beg him to stay. Hospitality to the stranger was required of the followers of Jesus. The Didache describes those requirements. One never knew if they were inviting a prophet or an angel of God into their home. Matthew tells us that welcoming a stranger was tantamount to welcoming Jesus himself (25:35). These two are portrayed as practicing Christian hospitality before the Christian community was formally defined.

Jesus accepts their invitation and, when asked to do the blessing, which was standard practice, they "recognize him in the breaking of the bread." He disappears and they immediately go back to the Apostles to tell them the Good News. We have to remember that, by now, it is night. It was dangerous to travel at night. Most people were afraid to travel at night. But these two are not afraid. They have seen the risen Christ and are filled with his presence. In a very real sense they had become apostles.

Now let me tell you the rest of the story. This wonderful story is also a metaphor for the Eucharistic celebration. We don't exactly know how the Eucharist was celebrated in the first century but it must have been somewhat similar to our present day celebrations.[32] The Catholic Church divides the Eucharist into four parts: "The Gathering", "The Liturgy of the Word", The Liturgy of the Eucharist" and "The Sending Forth". You'll notice that Luke's story contains all four of these parts. "The Gathering" occurs when the two people are gathered in the name of Jesus and Jesus said that whenever two or more are gathered in his name he is present. "The Liturgy of the Word" begins when the two unwittingly proclaim the Gospel and then Jesus explains the Scripture. "The Liturgy of the Eucharist", of course, is when Jesus breaks

---

32     In about 135 CE, Justin Martyr, a Church apologist, described the Eucharistic celebration in a way that is quite similar to the modern Eucharistic celebration. People gathered in a home. The President, i.e. Presider, of the assembly would lead them; the scripture was read and the Psalms sung. The President would then explain the readings and exhort the people to act accordingly. A collection was taken for the poor and then the consecrated bread and wine were distributed. Deacons would take them to the infirmed when the assembly was dismissed (First Apology, Chapter LXVI). It seems likely that Luke or an editor was aware of this structure, which, I believe also promotes a second century dating of the Gospel.

bread and "The Sending Forth" is when the two go back to the Apostles to tell them Jesus has been raised.

I'm sure that this relationship to the Eucharist was not accidental. "The Breaking of the Bread" was a regular ritual in the infant Church. After the destruction of the Jerusalem Temple in 70 **CE** it surely became the heart of Christian worship. I think Luke is reminding his/her audience that while they cannot physically see Jesus they can recognize his presence in the community through liturgy, most particularly through the celebration of the "Breaking of the Bread".

As I mentioned in the beginning of this Chapter, Luke/Acts is a literary gem. Powerful and memorable stories transmit a message that is filled with hope. They are stories which speak of the Gospel's humble beginnings with the birth of Jesus in a manger in the little town of Bethlehem; it ends with Paul freely proclaiming his powerful message in Rome, the center of the then known world. They are stories that speak of compassion and forgiveness. The words of Jesus resonate with the poor, the outcasts and the marginalized and at the same time severely indict the proud and the self-righteous. Behind all these words stands the Holy Spirit, the One who provides the words and the power. Praise God for the gift of the Spirit and thank God for Luke.

## LUKE'S JESUS

### The Glorious Lord

Since, Luke, by his/her own admission, used several written sources, his/her understanding of Jesus is not firsthand. If he were a disciple of Paul then his understanding of Jesus would have been as the glorified Lord who appeared to Paul on the road to Damascus. In some ways this seems to be the case. Luke is the only evangelist who refers to Jesus as "Lord". Paul refers to Jesus as Lord in every one of his letters. Luke's infancy narrative portrays the glory of the Lord shining about him at his birth. The transfiguration, rather than projecting the future glory of the resurrection, as in Mark and Matthew, seems to reflect the glory that was present from the beginning in Bethlehem. Unlike Mark, the Jesus of Luke is manifested more as the risen Lord than a son of man. This is because Luke only knew the risen Lord. He/she had never seen Jesus in the flesh. He/she was probably using sources that reflected experiences of Jesus in the Spirit rather than in the flesh.

## A King Forever

Jesus is also portrayed as a king. Luke is the only evangelist who states Jesus is clearly a king and he does it six times (1:32-33; 19:12, 28; 22:28, 67; 23:40). While Luke says that Jesus is the son of the Most High and that God will give him the throne of David and a Kingdom over which he will rule forever, his kingship is different from Mark's description. For Luke, Jesus is conceived by the Holy Spirit; the very breath of God is in him from the moment of his conception. Angels announce his birth. Unlike Mark, the phrase "Son of God" is not merely equivalent to the title, "Son of David". Rather it's an affirmation of his nature. I don't think Luke is saying that Jesus is the same as God, but like Paul, he is seen as greater than angels and a manifestation of God's presence on earth.

## The Humble Servant and Champion of the Marginalized

Luke's Jesus is also portrayed as a servant. He reflects the great hymn found in Philippians 2:6-7: "Who, though he was in the form of God, did not deem equality with God something to be grasped. Rather he emptied himself and took the form of a slave . . ." Though glorified, Jesus is still human reaching out to everyone but especially to those who are in need—the lowly, the poor and the marginalized. Like them "The Son of Man" has nowhere to rest his head" (9:58). He is also a friend of publicans and sinners (7:34). He associates with them because as he says, "Those who are healthy do not need a physician, but the sick do." (5:31). This possibly reflects the fact that Luke's community was comprised of the poor and outcasts, marginalized sinners who had repented and received the gift of salvation.

Luke's Jesus has close relationships with women. First century Israel often scorned women, especially those who were suspected of illicit behavior. Women had no rights, were not considered valid witnesses in a court of Law, normally did not own property and were basically seen as second-class citizens or even worse, property. Even in the Greco-Roman world, women, while more independent than Jewish women, were still subservient to men. In spite of this, Luke presents women as traveling companions of Jesus, not on a regular basis but they are often seen in the background. Mary, the sister of Martha, is presented sitting at Jesus' feet, an attitude of discipleship (10:39) and Mary Magdalene, Susanna and Joanna and other women financially supported Jesus' ministry. (8:2-3)

Jesus was criticized for associating with outcasts and women. One wonders why he often went beyond the boundaries of culturally acceptable behavior. Certainly Luke's message is that he came to bring salvation for all people; however, there must be more to it than that.

Perhaps his concern for the outcasts and the marginalized reflected the fact that, as a child, Jesus himself may have been outcast. Consider the conditions surrounding his birth. No one is going to believe Mary's story about the angel. Either, she and Joseph had sexual relations before they were formally married or Mary had another lover. Both were unacceptable and forbidden by Jewish law. As a result, Jesus would have been treated as someone conceived out of wedlock. This was a society that punished those who didn't conform. The neighbors would have rejected his mother. They would not have allowed their children to play with Jesus. His formal training in the synagogue could have been limited. In other words, Jesus may have felt the sting of being treated as an outcast. He would have known the pain of not being accepted and therefore, as an adult, could easily relate to the marginalized. In the same way, he would have seen the pain his mother endured and, as a result, been more open to women who were mistreated because they didn't conform to the accepted norms of their society.

## The Perfect Human Being

Luke's Jesus is also a model of the perfect man. Jesus is what all of us can be if we do as he has done and live as he has lived. As the Holy Spirit embraced Jesus, Acts tells us that every believer receives the same Spirit. Because we are filled with the Spirit, like Jesus, we too can proclaim the Gospel, work miracles, and be a friend of the poor and the lowly. Jesus is the model upon which every believer should pattern his life. As he was transfigured so we too are transformed by the Spirit because as Acts 16:7 and Phil. 1:19 tell us, this Spirit is the Spirit of Jesus.

Luke's Jesus is a person who prays often. All the Gospels tell us that Jesus prayed but Luke tells us that he prayed all night at times. (5:16; 6:12; 9:28) His way of praying apparently impressed his disciples so much that they asked him to teach them how to pray (11:1).

## Conclusion

So, in conclusion, Luke's Jesus is the manifestation of the Divine in and through the perfect man who everyone must imitate and follow. He is the Lord who rules and yet the lowly one who serves. He is compassionate but demanding. We cannot take his message lightly. We must choose him and commit ourselves entirely to his good news. He is the one who brings joy to the world but that joy comes from our faith in him, a faith that transforms us because through the power of the Spirit he lives in us.

## PERSONAL REFLECTION

The Parable of the Rich man and Lazarus (16:19-31) is unique to Luke. It reflects the Lucan theme of care for the poor and the marginalized. Lazarus is covered with sores which implies that he is a leper. Lepers were not allowed to be in public. They were usually confined to colonies away from populated areas. Therefore, he is an outcast. The rich man is dressed in purple garments, a sign of great wealth. They both die and Lazarus is in heaven and the rich man is in hell.

The story is a polemic against those who are wealthy. I don't think Luke condemns wealth per se. He/she condemns those who ignore the needs of the poor and don't charitably use their wealth. He/she condemns those who look down on the less fortunate. So the story is about greed and arrogance.

According to the standards of the world, I am wealthy. I'm not a millionaire but I certainly have enough money to care for the needs of myself and my family. I certainly have enough money to live a very comfortable life. This story makes me question my values. How important are the poor? Do I discriminate against any ethnic or religious groups? Do I discriminate against those I judge to be sinful or those who believe differently than I do? Am I attached to my money? Does money interfere with my relationship with God, myself and others? Do I hoard my money or do I share it graciously with others? These are tough questions and quite frankly I have to say that I must answer yes to some of them.

Luke 12:33-34 tells us that where our treasure is so is our heart. He/she goes on to say that we need to store our treasure in heaven where no one can take it away. After all, we are only here for a short time. No matter how many possessions we have we need to realize that someday all of them will belong to someone else. No one ever drags a U-Haul behind a hearse! What's strange is that no matter how much money people have most of them think they need more. We all need to change our thinking when it comes to money. We need to store our treasure in heaven, not on earth.

The story of Lazarus and the rich man in essence says that we need to keep our priorities straight. Money is important. We need it to provide for our needs but we also have to realize that our relationships with people are more important. We cannot ignore the needs of the poor. We cannot pass judgment on those who are different than we are. If we dare to call ourselves Christian then we must be merciful; to realize that is not legalism and ritual, that God desires. It's mercy.

# Chapter Three

# THE GOSPEL OF MATTHEW

The Gospel of Matthew is listed first in the New Testament. One reason is because it was thought to have been written before any of the others. Another reason may have been because it focuses so strongly on the Kingdom of God and its manifestation in the Church. It is the only Gospel to use the word *ecclesia*, the Greek word for Church (16:18 and 18:17). Hence it has been called the Gospel of the Church and, as such was held in high regard by the Roman Catholic Church. In fact, prior to the liturgical changes in the Catholic Church in the late 60's, except for a few instances, the Gospel of Matthew was the only Gospel read at the Tridentine (Latin) Mass.

As I mentioned earlier, Matthew, at least in its present form, must have been written after Mark because it uses Mark as its primary source.

Matthew is also the most Jewish of the four Gospels. He has 43 direct quotes from the Old Testament and refers to Old Testament passages over 130 times. He always refers to the Kingdom of God as the Kingdom of Heaven because of the Jewish sensitivity to pronouncing the name of God.[33]

---

[33] Jews were never allowed to pronounce the name of God, the name given to Moses at the burning bush. The name is recorded in the Hebrew Scriptures as YHWH, which is pronounced "Yahweh". Only the High Priest was allowed to pronounce the name of God and then only in the Holy of Holies, the inner sanctum of the Temple. He normally did this on the Day of Atonement. We're not absolutely sure of the pronunciation because this was reserved for the High Priest. Jews even refrained from using other names for God, such as "El" or "Elohim". The most common reference to God was "The Lord".

Matthew's Jesus often refers to the LAW[34], which is the Law of Moses and he uses casuistic or legalistic arguments to make his point.

Numbers are also very important in Matthew. Numerology was commonly practiced among the first century Jews and therefore, numbers had special meaning. For instance, the number seven referred to completion or perfection. Six represented evil, twelve, Israel and four, the world. It's hard to tell whether Matthew uses his numbers symbolically or simply as a memory device. He often puts his material in groups of three or seven. For example, there may be seven petitions, three parables, three tithes, three good works, etc.

## WHO WROTE IT?

When we consider all of the factors mentioned above it's easy to conclude that this Gospel was most likely written by a Jew for Jewish Christians. The author historically has been Matthew the Apostle. Papias said that Matthew wrote down the sayings of Jesus in his own language. However, the Gospel contains a lot more than the sayings of Jesus and it is written in Greek not Aramaic or Hebrew. Also, internal evidence indicates the Gospel was written sometime around 85 **C.E.** While it's possible Matthew could still have been alive then it's highly unlikely. We have to remember that the title says, "The Gospel *According* to Matthew." *According to* could indicate that Matthew the Apostle was the underlying source for the Gospel. After all, the Gospel contains a lot more sayings of Jesus than Mark or Luke. In fact, as I mentioned earlier, the Q document may well have been Matthew's sayings Gospel.

Whoever wrote Matthew was probably a Hellenized Jew meaning that he did not live in Palestine and was culturally a Greek. He was well aware of the Old Testament and only quoted the Septuagint, which was the Greek translation of the Hebrew Scriptures.

---

[34] When I insert the word "LAW" as all capital letters it refers to the first five books of the Hebrew Scriptures. The Jews called these five books, "Torah" which literally means instruction. The Jews deem these five books the most sacred and traditionally Moses was credited as their author (since disproven) and so sometimes they are referred to as "The Law of Moses".

## DATE OF COMPOSITION

The Evangelist most likely wrote his Gospel, in its present form, somewhere between 85 and 90 **C.E.** I say that because it is quite obvious the author was well aware of the destruction of Jerusalem which occurred in 70 **C.E.** Canonical Mark also had time to circulate and be available to him. Perhaps the most important reason to date the Gospel so late is that the Evangelist's community is experiencing what is known as the Synagogue expulsions, which didn't occur until the 80's **C.E.** It's certainly possible that there was a proto Gospel, perhaps even written by Matthew the Apostle. As I said earlier, the Gospels probably went through several edits before taking their present form.

## BACKGROUND

Aside from the Christians, the Pharisees were the only large religious group to survive the destruction of Jerusalem. The Pharisees were extremely holy men who followed the letter of the Law of Moses. In fact, they often went beyond the letter of the LAW. Like Jesus and the early Christians they believed in life after death. They believed that if enough people would follow their way of life the Messiah would come. One of the main differences between them and the Christians was that they believed good works put them right with God. In other words, they felt they could earn their way into heaven.

After the destruction of the Temple, they met at Jamnia, a town near present day Tel Aviv, and decided that since there was no longer a Temple, Judaism had to be re-defined. They unified synagogue worship and devised a new liturgical calendar. Some years later they determined the Old Testament Canon. They also tried to understand why God allowed the destruction of their Temple and the desecration of the holy city of Jerusalem by pagans. Their conclusion was sectarian groups had polluted Judaism and, because of this, God had punished them. Since Christianity was essentially the only sectarian group to survive, the Pharisees devised ways to get rid of them. One way was to prevent Christians from participating in synagogue worship. A petition was introduced into a Jewish prayer, which was called the Eighteen Benedictions. It cited heretics, apostates and Christians who were referred to as "the proud". This obviously caused a great deal of conflict between Christians and Jews even to the point where Jews physically threw the Christians out of the Synagogue. Since this didn't occur until the early 80's **C.E.** and Matthew is aware of it, his Gospel had to be written around that time or afterwards.

When trying to understand the Gospel of Matthew we must understand that his community was engaged in an ongoing feud with the Pharisees. The tension between Jesus and the Pharisees in Matthew was really a reflection of the tension between Matthew's community and the Pharisees who reformed Judaism. The Pharisees were constantly challenging the leaders of Matthew's community regarding their belief that Jesus was the Messiah. They challenged them about their interpretation of the Law of Moses. No doubt St Paul influenced their thinking and we know most orthodox Jews, which surely included some Pharisees, hated Paul (Acts 23:12-15).

In the flesh, Jesus probably had a limited amount of conflict with the Pharisees. I'm sure they had some differences of opinion but they were in agreement far more than not. As we shall see in Matthew, Jesus, like the Pharisees, followed the Law of Moses. He even says that he will not change even the slightest part of the Law (5:17-18). The Sermon on the Mount indicates that, like the Pharisees, Jesus expected his followers to go beyond the LAW. However, the real difference between Jesus and the Pharisees is that Jesus placed far more emphasis on one's intentions rather than his actions: on what is in one's heart rather than on his resume so to speak.

Matthew's Jesus is most likely much more confrontational with the Pharisees than Jesus in the flesh. His community was primarily composed of Christian Jews. They did not envision themselves as a people separate from Judaism. They were simply Jews who believed that Jesus was the Messiah and would return in glory to establish his kingdom. The Pharisees basically gave them an ultimatum. Either they renounce Jesus or they would be ostracized from the synagogue. This created a great deal of anxiety because they had strong ties to the mother faith and often attended synagogue services. But they also felt compelled to follow Jesus. No doubt families were divided by the decision of some to stay Christian and others who returned to the mother religion.

The community turned to their prophets to guide them. Christian prophets spoke for Christ. They believed that Christ spoke through them via the power and presence of the Holy Spirit. It was the way Jesus kept his promise that he would always be with them. As a result, they would turn to Jesus for guidance especially regarding new problems that arose. We shall see later that John's Gospel is more a proclamation of Jesus received through prophetic revelation than the Jesus of history. The Jesus we see in Matthew is often different from the Jesus in the flesh because the issues were different. So it's safe to say Matthew's Gospel is primarily a response to issues with the reformed Judaism of the Pharisees and the effect it had on his community.

Additionally, some believe Matthew's Gospel, because of its demand to not only obey Mosaic Law but also go beyond it, is a polemic against St. Paul's doctrine of salvation by faith. While it might be very interesting to have Paul and Matthew in the same room, Paul's big issue was circumcision, a point that Matthew never addresses. I think in many ways Paul would agree with Matthew but he would say that true faith in Jesus and the presence of the Holy Spirit empowers a person to live according to the fulfilled law dictated by Matthew's Jesus.

## HIGHLIGHTS AND THEMES

Matthew's Gospel is divided into three parts: 1) the infancy narrative, 2) Jesus' ministry and teaching and 3) the passion, death and resurrection. Like Mark, his main purpose is to demonstrate that Jesus is the Messiah, the Son of God but Matthew does this a bit differently. He wants to portray Jesus as a new Moses who fulfills the LAW and establishes his Kingdom, i.e. "the new and everlasting covenant" which is manifested in the Church.

### The Infancy Narrative (1:18-2:23)

As I mentioned in my commentary on the Gospel of Luke, Matthew's story regarding the birth of Jesus is quite different than Luke's story. His main focus is on Joseph rather than Mary. Instead of the shepherds he gives us the Magi. Herod plays a major role in Matthew and of course he adds the star of Bethlehem, the story of the slaughter of the innocents and the flight into Egypt.

However, some of the information is similar. Both Gospels indicate Joseph and Mary are the parents of Jesus albeit Joseph his paternal father. Both tell us Jesus was born in Bethlehem during the reign of King Herod the Great and that Jesus' family ended up living in Nazareth. Both tell us Mary conceived Jesus through the power of the Holy Spirit and Matthew makes it clear that Mary and Joseph "had no sexual relations until Mary gave birth to a son" (1:25). Both say Jesus is a son of David but they give us totally different genealogies.

As we said earlier, these stories are far more theological than historical. Matthew has an agenda whereby he wants to portray Jesus as a new Moses who has come not only for the Jews but also for the Gentiles. As Moses was spared from the wrath of Pharaoh, so Jesus is spared from the wrath of Herod. As Moses went down into Egypt and then came out of Egypt so too Jesus went down into Egypt and also came out of Egypt. But Jesus is greater than Moses because, unlike Moses, he crossed the Jordan and went into the Promised Land.

King Herod's rejection of Jesus symbolizes the Jewish leaders' rejection of him and more importantly the Synagogue leaders who are persecuting Matthew's community. The story of the Magi contrasts this rejection. They are pagans and yet they recognize Jesus as a king and bow down before him and pay him homage. As much as the leaders of the Jews are rejecting Jesus in the 80's **C.E.** the Gentiles are accepting him.


## The Genealogy (1:1-17)

If you compare Matthew's genealogy to Luke's you also find significant differences. Luke traces Jesus' ancestry backwards to Adam; Matthew starts with Abraham. Luke does this to show that the salvation Jesus offers is universal; no one is excluded. Matthew is interested in showing that Jesus is Jewish.[35] Notice that the names are different from David to Joseph. Scholars have tried to reconcile the differences but quite unsuccessfully. Catholic scholars in the past contended that the genealogy in Luke is really Mary's line, however, Luke 3:23 clearly ends with Joseph not Mary. Here, again we must understand that we are not dealing with history but theology. Matthew, for instance, divides his genealogy into three sets of fourteen generations. Remember, numerology seems to be important to Matthew. If you add up the numerical value for the name David in Hebrew the sum is fourteen. The number three symbolizes perfection. So, one could conclude that Matthew's genealogy was devised to show that Jesus is the culmination of the Davidic line, the perfect descendant who is Messiah and Son of God.

---

[35] By the time Matthew wrote his Gospel a rumor was circulating that Jesus was illegitimate. This rumor, meant to debase the virginal conception and Jesus' ancestry, stated that a Roman soldier, Pantarus, raped Mary and that Jesus was conceived as a result. Matthew may be responding to that via his genealogy.

## THE SERMON ON THE MOUNT (5-7)

The *Sermon on the Mount*, without a doubt is the most extraordinary compendium of Jesus' teachings and therefore requires a lot of attention. Partial parallels are found in Luke 6:20-49. The Epistle of James records a few of these sayings but they are not placed on the lips of Jesus. The *Didache* contains a number of these sayings as well.

I think the majority of scholars would agree Jesus never said these words on a single occasion. Most likely, Matthew collected the sayings of Jesus, which were primarily found in "Q", and added more material from other traditions. He then placed them in an orderly fashion and created a single testimony that basically summarizes the essential teachings of Jesus at least from Matthew's perspective.

Remember, Matthew is presenting Jesus as the new Moses. In this case, Jesus like Moses presents the new law but, instead of going up the mountain alone as Moses did, Jesus brings the people with him and gives them the new fulfilled Mosaic Law. This is also the first of five discourses; the number five being significant since these discourses could represent the first five books of the Hebrew Scripture, i.e. *Torah*, which legend says was written by Moses.

The sermon begins with the nine beatitudes (blessings). Four are mentioned in Luke. Most likely, Matthew either added the other five or he drew from a different version of Q. One might try to view these nine statements as a parallel to the Ten Commandments; however, they are not commandments as such. They are simply blessings for those who belong to the Kingdom of Heaven. I suppose one could divide them up into three sets of three to indicate that numerologically they are the ultimate and most perfect teaching, even greater than the Decalogue. Whether Matthew had that in mind there is no way of knowing. They are certainly meant to describe those who are indeed the fortunate (another translation for blessed) in the eyes of God.

Notice how they contradict the ways of the world. Through secular eyes, poverty, meekness, hunger and even mercy are not attributes one needs to get ahead especially in the temporal or political scene. However, Jesus often uses what is known as the rule of reversal to make his point. For instance, Jesus tells us in all four Gospels that the last will be first and that if we want to be leaders we must first become slaves. *The Beatitudes* are another way of saying this. It seems apparent that the majority of those who followed Jesus were the marginalized; people who had little wealth and no social status. The educated and wealthy had little time for Jesus and his followers because the concepts of letting go of material things and social standing was not only something they wouldn't do but also concepts that didn't make sense to them.

The last beatitude was probably directed to the disciples as well as the leaders in Matthew's community. Suffering and even dying for the sake of the Gospel was commonplace in the early Church. Steven was the first to be martyred in the early 30's **C.E.**, then James the Apostle in about 44 **C.E.** James the brother of Jesus was bludgeoned to death in about 62 **C.E.** Peter and Paul were martyred in about 65 **C.E.** and of course many others were arrested, scourged or stoned.

Still directing his attention to the disciples, Matthew's Jesus calls them the "salt of the earth and the light of the world" (5:13-14). They are the ones who are to flavor the earth with the Gospel. They must not allow their message to lose its taste[36] and they must not keep the light of truth hidden because this is the way people will learn the Good News and give glory to God.

Verses 5:17-7:28 magnifies Matthew's presentation of Jesus as the new Moses. Here begins a direct comparison of Jesus' teaching to the Law of Moses or "Torah" as the Jews called it. Actually, Jesus refers to the "LAW and the Prophets", which encompasses the entire Hebrew Scriptures. He begins by saying that he's not going to change even the smallest part of the LAW[37] but then he's goes ahead and changes it! But he changes it by making it more demanding. Notice the formula used, "You have heard it said to your ancestors . . . but I say unto you . . ." Jesus quotes "Torah" and then

---

36    The line, "but what if the salt loses its taste" has long mystified readers. Salt never loses its taste. Apparently, people in biblical Israel cooked in large pots and they would place a bag of course unrefined salt in the broth to season it. They used it over and over until all the salt dissolved leaving the insoluble minerals behind. They would then throw them out to be "trampled underfoot."

37    The literal translation of "not the smallest letter or the smallest part of a letter" is "not a jot or a tittle". Ancient Hebrew was written using only consonants. There was also no punctuation, which made it very difficult to read and understand. Later, small marks were made above or below a consonant to help the reader know which word was actually meant. This usage is found in the Dead Sea Scrolls. A "Jot" in Hebrew is *yod* the smallest letter in the alphabet. "Tittles" are the marks by the letters. A good example is the Red Sea. Transliterated into English it would simply be "RD". Scholars now realized that it was not the Red Sea the Israelites crossed but a marshy area to the north called the *Reed* Sea.

gives a new and more difficult version. Murder is a sin but now anger can be just as sinful (5:22). Adultery is an evil but now even a lustful glance is evil (5:28). Divorce was acceptable under the LAW but now divorce is not allowed (5:32). Even taking an oath (55:33) and retaliating against an attacker (5:39) is considered to be unacceptable for the believer.

By using this formula Matthew elevates Jesus to a position, which is not only greater than Moses but also one, which makes him almost divine. Who would dare change the Law of Moses, a law that was given to the Israelites by God? I don't think Matthew is saying that Jesus is the same as God. This would have been the utmost blasphemy, which would certainly not help his cause with the leaders of the Jews or even Jewish Christians. Yet, while the Jews demanded an adherence to the notion of one God, they did believe that creatures were given divine powers. Good examples would be angels and prophets like Moses. That Jesus was such a person is a given for Matthew. I'm not saying that Jesus wasn't divine only that this notion was a later development.

The sermon continues with powerful statements, which tell us to love our enemies and to pray for our persecutors (5:43-45). Jesus tells us prayer is not about the sheer repetition of words or for show. True prayer comes from the heart and is the recognition of God's supreme authority (6:5-8). The Our Father is provided as an example. Notice how much simpler Luke's version is (Luke 11:3-4). Matthew, again has either embellished "Q" or he is using a different source.[38]

For me, the most beautiful and compelling passages in the Sermon are 6:24-34, which remind us of God's concern for those who love God. God will provide for us if only we believe that God wants what's best for us and loves us more than we could ever imagine.

Chapter seven concludes the Sermon with warnings against judging others (7:1-5) followed by more instruction about the power of prayer, (7:7-11) the golden rule, (7:12) the danger of false prophets (7:21-23)[39] and that one must be a doer of the Word of God not just a hearer (7:24-27).

---

[38] Another version is found in the Didache. It is virtually identical to Matthew's Our Father but it adds the now familiar ending, "The Kingdom, the power and the glory are yours . . . "

[39] The rise of false prophets was a problem even in Paul's time and would continue to be a problem for centuries. It would take quite a while before the Church could iron out the issues. Some are still there! Matthew's main point here is

Judging others is a particularly important theme in Matthew. The way in which we judge others is the rule God will use to judge us (7:2). This is also true of forgiveness. If we do not forgive others God will not forgive us. Every time we say the Lord's Prayer we say, "Forgive us our trespasses as we forgive those who trespass against us" (6:12).

The Sermon ends with parable-like story of building one's house on rock rather than sand. The teachings of Jesus provide the sturdy foundation on which every believer must shape his or her faith. Actually, Jesus himself is the rock and the cornerstone (See 1 Pet. 2:4-8).

Some feel that the demands made by Jesus in the Sermon on the Mount are idealistic and reserved for the perfect disciple if there is such a person. While the material may seem idealistic, the Jesus we find in the Gospels was not. He was a realist who had a soft spot in his heart for the poor and the outcast, for the suffering and the sinner. I don't think that Jesus would present a formula for living that he really didn't think we could follow.

Matthew, on the other hand, may have embellished Jesus' words to demonstrate that Jesus was even more demanding than the Pharisees. Of course, this is only conjecture but I'm convinced the evangelist doctored the words of Jesus to fit the needs of his community. We often see this when we compare the Synoptic Gospels side-by-side.

I believe that the main import of this Sermon has to do with intent more than action, with what's in one's heart rather than what one says he believes. For instance, if we really believe that murder is an evil we will do nothing that would occasion the possibility of murder, e.g. anger. If we are truly persons of integrity, people would never demand that we swear what we say is true. If we truly believe peace is the answer to many of the world's problems than retaliation is not an option. If we don't believe some of them then we must not say we do or pretend to follow them like some of the Pharisees. If we are to be the salt of the earth and the light of the world then we must not do things which give bad example and we must be totally committed to living out the Gospel.

---

that it's not enough to simply believe in Jesus or call him your Lord. True discipleship, as the Sermon indicates, requires much more. This teaching is contrary to the teachings of St Paul and to some which are found the Gospel of John. However, contrary is not always a bad thing. It can provide a balance, which is often required to put things into their proper perspective.

If we fail to live out these precepts we must not give up the quest to live them to the fullest. The true believer will forgive us our trespasses and God will forgive them as well. It is far better to try than to simply write them off as an impossible dream. Finally, we must never dismiss the power of grace. As St. Paul would say, "For by grace you have been saved through faith, and this is not from you; it is a gift from God" (Eph. 2:8).

## MATTHEW'S PARABLES

Like Luke, Matthew's Jesus teaches using long parables, which, like Luke, have been allegorized. Some he shares in common with Luke but others are unique to Matthew. These include: the parable of the seed growing slowly (4:26-29), the parable of the weeds (13:24-30), the parable of the net 13:47-50), the parable of the householder (13:51-52), the parable of the unmerciful servant (18:23-35), the parable of the workers in the vineyard (20:1-16), the parable of the two sons (21:28-31) and the parable of the ten maidens (25:1-13).

Chapter 13, often called Jesus' third great discourse, is devoted to parables about the Kingdom of Heaven and the Church. All find parallels in Mark and Luke until verse 36 where Matthew introduces new material, beginning with an explanation of the parable of the weeds and wheat, and ends with Jesus challenging his disciples by asking them if they really understand the meaning of the Kingdom of Heaven.

### The Laborers in the Vineyard (20:1-16)

This Parable provides an example of the ways of the Kingdom. The householder goes into the market place to hire workers to come to his vineyard to pick grapes. This is taking place in the fall of the year when the grapes are ripening. Usually the vineyard owner will wait as long as he possibly can so that the grapes will have high sugar content. He can't wait too long, however, because the rainy season is near and once that starts he will not be able to pick all the grapes. We are told in the parable that he goes to the town early in the morning and promises the workers that he will pay them a full day's wage. Then he goes back several more times and hires more workers so that the last to be hired only work for about an hour.

At the end of the day he decides to pay everyone a full day's wage which causes the ones who worked the whole day to grumble: "These last ones worked only one hour and you have made them equal to us, who bore the day's burden and the heat" (20:12). But the landowners replies, "Am I not free to do what I want with my money?" (20:15).

The main point of this parable echoes the words of Jesus when he says, "The last shall be first and the first shall be last," indicating that in the Kingdom of God everyone will be treated equally. One cannot earn God's love because whether we are good or bad God wants what is best for us. That's the meaning of divine love. People will enter the kingdom in many different ways and at different stages of their lives but the reward will be the same—eternal life. The story of the good thief (Luke 23:43-43) gives witness to this.

## The Wedding Feast (22:1-14)

This parable is found in both Matthew and Luke (Lk 14:15-24) and, as such, is probably from Q. However, Matthew's version adds additional material and a different ending. Both have been allegorized: Matthew's version more so than Luke's. In Matthew's parable, the King represents God, the son is Jesus, the servants are the prophets and/or the apostles and the feast is the Messianic Banquet.[40] Those who were initially invited were the Jewish people, particularly their leaders. The ones who are gathered from the streets probably represent the members of Matthew's community, and other members of the Christian Churches including the poor, the outcasts and the marginalized of the Greco-Roman world. Most of the Jews and their leaders have rejected the Gospel message and from Matthew's perspective, God has punished them by destroying their city, Jerusalem, and killing many of its inhabitants. Here the Roman emperor, Titus, is depicted as God's

---

[40]  As we have seen, the early Church believed that when Jesus returned to establish his Kingdom the entire Church would somehow gather together for a great banquet. They would sit at the table of the Lord and feast with him. The love feast or agape meal was celebrated in Paul's communities. The assembly would gather and everyone, rich and poor, would eat a great meal and then celebrate Eucharist at the end. Symbolically, the meal prefigured the Messianic Banquet that was to come.

emissary. Titus was the General who, with his army, destroyed the city and it's Temple in 70 **CE.**

Matthew's message is clear. Those who were first called, the Jews, will not share in the Messianic banquet. Rather it will be the outcasts of society and, even those who are Gentiles, will receive the promise of salvation.

The idea that God punished the Jews and destroyed their city because they rejected Jesus is disturbing to most of us. "Would a loving God do such a thing?" we ask. We must remember the Jews believed that in some way God was responsible for everything. Nothing, good or bad, could happen without God's willing it. The Pharisees blamed the Christians and other sectarian Jews for the destruction of Jerusalem. They had polluted the faith with their heretical teachings. As a result, Christians could no longer worship in the Synagogue. Conversely, Christians, as we see in this parable, responded by saying the Jews were being punished because they rejected Jesus. They both believed that God had a hand in all this and that God must have a logical reason for either doing or allowing it. The long term repercussions have been enormous. Jews and Christians have been at odds for two millennia mainly because of these words. This is why it is so important to understand the words of Scripture in their context.

Matthew's parable ends with a strange story about the man without a wedding garment. The judgment here seems totally unfair. After all, the man was gathered by the servants and brought to the feast. He was probably poor and couldn't afford to properly dress for the occasion. So why punish him?

Actually, the story is about baptism. The baptized, after they came out of the waters of baptism, were clothed in a white garment as a sign of their newfound dignity and, that they had figuratively put on Christ as Paul says in Gal. 3:27. Baptism was a right of initiation required of all who wished to belong to the Church. Baptism opened to doorway to receiving the Holy Spirit. It was mandatory if one wished to participate in the life of the Church. In short, if you aren't baptized you can't belong, period! The pericope may reflect an issue between the Jewish Christians and the Gentiles in Matthew's community. The Jewish Christians may have felt circumcision and belief in Jesus was all that was required, whereas the Gentiles, who were more in tune with Paul's teachings, believed baptism actually replaced circumcision.

If you compare this with Luke's version you find that Luke's is much simpler. There is no mention of the destruction of Jerusalem and no story about the wedding garment. For Luke the message is simply that the poor and the lowly have accepted the message while the rest of society made excuses and turned down the invitation. As a result they will not receive the promise of salvation.

This a good example of how two Evangelists will draw from the same source, in this case Q, and retell the story to suit their agenda. Luke's version, since it is shorter and simpler, is probably closer to the original. His source may have been written before the destruction of Jerusalem, whereas Matthew's was obviously after it. As a result, Matthew stylized the story and added material to address issues in his community. The important point I'm making here is that stories in the Scripture do not have to be historically accurate or in agreement with each other to be the inspired Word of God. It's the message that counts.

## The Parable of the Two Sons (21:28-32)

The Parable of the Two Sons is also a message about the Kingdom of Heaven. Here again we have an allegory, wherein the first son represents the leaders of the Jewish people and the second son, sinners. The man is either Jesus or God. This story is similar to Luke's story of the Prodigal Son; wherein the younger son represents the sinner and the elder son the righteous.

The message here is similar to the parable of the wedding feast discussed above. The Scribes and the Pharisees have rejected the Gospel but those who initially rejected the message, i.e. publicans and prostitutes, have now accepted it. They are members of the Kingdom of Heaven while the so-called righteous ones are outside the Kingdom.

Then Matthew's Jesus adds a postscript, which tells us that those who followed John the Baptizer were the same kinds of people who have accepted the Gospel of Jesus. This confirms that many of John's followers became followers of Jesus. The Gospel of John tells us some of John's disciples were numbered among the twelve apostles. See John 1:35-51.

## SOME OTHER PASSAGES UNIQUE TO MATTHEW

Aside from some of the parables and a portion of the Sermon on the Mount material, there are several other episodes which are only found in Matthew. They include: Matthew 10:17-25, Mathew 23:1-36 and Matthew 25:31-46.

## The Coming Persecution (10:16-36)

Matthew 10:16-36 reflects persecutions that are taking place or took place, not only in his community but also in others as well. The persecution in question was probably by the Pharisees in Matthew's community but the Romans also disliked the Christians. Nero's persecution, which took place in the mid 60's **CE,** would not have been successful if this were not the case. This helps to explain vss. 21 and 22, which describes division with the family and a general hatred by those outside the Church. When the Pharisees demanded that Christians deny Jesus and return to the mother religion, some family members did while others did not. This would obviously cause division among family members since nothing divides people more than religion and politics.

This was also a problem in the Gentile Churches. Once a person became a Christian he could no longer eat with his pagan family since they ate meat sacrificed to idols. He could not go to the games because they were considered too violent. Certainly, they couldn't attend the orgy-like parties because the Church deemed them immoral. They couldn't offer sacrifices to the pagan gods, which upset their pagan family. Most Romans and Greeks were very superstitious. Their gods provided them with health and protection. Christians would not offer sacrifices to their gods, which the Romans believed made them angry and an irate god might take out his anger on them or the entire city. In fact, this was probably the main reason that the pagans persecuted the Christians. So it's easy to see how Jesus' words reflect what is taking place in the Church of the 80's **CE.**

Vs. 19 is also reflected in Luke 12:11-12 which says, "When they take you before the synagogues or before rulers and authorities, do not worry about what you are to say. The Holy Spirit will teach you at that moment what you should say." John 14:26 provides a similar parallel, "The Advocate, the Holy Spirit that the Father will send in my name—he will teach you everything and remind you all that I told you."

As I mentioned before, the Church used a prophetic model. There was no hierarchical structure until the second century. The Holy Spirit governed it. Presbyters, Deacons, Prophets, etc. were chosen by the Holy Spirit as the community prayed over them. Everyone received the Spirit when they were baptized and the apostles laid hands on them. As on the day of Pentecost, "They all were filled with the Holy Spirit" (Acts.2:4). Consequently, the Church believed that the Spirit would guide and council them especially during the stressful times of persecution.

The last verse of this pericope is mysterious. Matthew's Jesus can't be talking about the Parousia, i.e. the Last Judgment, because, by the 90's **CE,** the Gospel would have been proclaimed throughout Galilee and Jesus still hadn't returned. Perhaps this part of the discourse refers to the end of a disciple's life when, as John 14:3 Jesus says, "I will come back again and take you to myself."

## Denunciation of the Scribes and Pharisees (23:1-36)

There are no parallel verses in any of the other four Gospels that compare with the scathing condemnation of the Pharisees found in Matthew 23. Several times Matthew's Jesus calls them hypocrites (23:15, 25 and 29). He lists a series of seven woes, (23:13-29) which again focuses on their hypocrisy. The word "woe" is often found in apocalyptic and prophetic literature and is meant to express horror for the sins one has committed. It is here that Jesus calls them "whitewashed tombs, which appear beautiful on the outside, but inside are full of dead man's bones and every kind of filth" (23:27).

Actually, this indictment of the Pharisees is quite unfair. The Pharisees, which numbered about 6000 men, were probably the holiest people in Israel. They obeyed the Mosaic Law to the letter and added their own laws as a means to better fulfill the LAW. For example, the LAW said that one could not work on the Sabbath but did not spell out exactly what one was allowed to do before it was deemed work. The Pharisees clarified this. At times this put them at odds with Jesus. When Jesus took mud on the Sabbath and placed it over the blind man's eyes, (John 9:6) the Pharisees said that he had broken the Sabbath—not according to Mosaic Law but according to the extended law of the Pharisees. This was a bone of contention between Jesus and the Pharisees. For Jesus, compassion superseded the LAW and the LAW was not meant to enslave people but rather to provide a guide for them to lead a life that was acceptable to God. "The sabbath was made for man, not man for the sabbath" (Mark 2:27). I think it is accurate to say that Jesus and the Pharisees were probably in agreement on nearly all other matters.

Most likely it is not the Jesus in the flesh who said these words. As I mentioned above, the Pharisees had redefined Judaism after the destruction of the Temple. In the process of doing that they condemned the Christians as heretics and, at times, even bodily threw them out of the Synagogues. They constantly challenged the Christian's claim that Jesus was the Messiah and demanded scriptural proof to back up that claim. In effect, they made life miserable for the Churches of the 80's and 90's **CE**. So, what we hear in chapter 23 is not the response of Jesus in the flesh but Matthew's Jesus responding to the Pharisees who are badgering Matthew's community.


## The Judgment of the Nations (25:31-46)

One of the most well-known pericopes is Matthew's dissertation regarding the last judgment. Here Jesus tells us the Son of Man will one day judge all the nations of the world. He will separate them into sheep and goats and the blessed (the sheep) will inherit the Kingdom while the unrighteous (the goats) will be cast into the fires of hell.

What makes this pericope unique are the conditions Jesus prescribes as necessary for salvation. He tells them when they feed the hungry, clothed the naked, visit the imprisoned, etc. they are doing these deeds to Jesus himself. This is not surprising since the early Church saw themselves as the body of Christ. However, this is in stark contrast with the teachings of St Paul, who makes it clear that we are not saved by works or by obedience to the Law of Moses; rather we are saved by faith in Jesus Christ and the grace that comes from it (Gal 2:16; Eph. 2:8-9). John's Jesus confirms this when he says salvation comes from believing in him (John 3:18).

Yet here, the righteous ones are not necessarily believers. They don't realize that their good works are being done for or to Jesus. They don't recognize Jesus in the body of believers. So, in this case, faith has little or nothing to do with salvation. It's their works that are important.

This is a key passage because I believe it is telling us that non-Christians can attain eternal life. Prior to the Second Vatican Council, the Catholic Church basically said that only Catholics could go to heaven. Today, fundamentalist Christians claim that only those who believe in Jesus Christ can go to heaven. I think this passage from Matthew says that people can come to know Christ in their hearts and carry out his work by their care and concern for the poor, the sick and the lowly and, even though it's done unwittingly, it will lead to their salvation.

This is also an excellent example of how one sacred author can contradict another. However, contradiction is not a bad thing. It simply gives us a different perspective, one that is conditioned by the needs of a particular community. Matthew's community is probably the most Jewish of the communities that fostered the Gospels. Obviously, the focus is going to be more on obedience of the LAW since this teaching is central to Judaism. This doesn't deny the importance of faith in Jesus; rather it provides a means of living out one's faith. I'm certain St Paul would never say that caring for the poor, the sick and the imprisoned is not a good thing. He would simply say that this is the result of one's faith and an obvious one at that.

## MATTHEW'S PASSION (26-27)

With a few exceptions Matthew copied almost all of Mark's passion narrative. In addition to Mark's account he states that the High Priest's name was Caiaphas. John mentions Caiaphas as well. He was the son-in-law of Annas, also mentioned by John, who was the High Priest during Jesus' youth.

Matthew's Jesus criticizes the apostle who cut off the High Priest's servant's ear saying he could easily call upon "twelve legions of angels to save him" if needed (26:52-53. The evangelist probably interjected these verses because they were consistent with Jesus' pacifistic posture in this Gospel.

Matthew is the only Gospel that mentions Judas' suicide. Acts 2:18-19 briefly alludes to it but the story is different than Matthew's. He says Judas hanged himself (27:5). The account in Acts says he jumped off a cliff. They both say the money was used to buy a small cemetery, which was called, "Field of Blood".

Matthew's passion account is also unique because he is the only evangelist who tells the story of Pilate washing his hands. Notice how the dream motif that we saw in the infancy narratives in introduced here with Pilate's wife. In 27:24 Pilate declares his innocence and Matthew places the guilt squarely on the Jews. In 27:25 the Jewish people make the well-known statement, "Let his blood be on us and on our children." This is unfortunate for it has been used as the basis for anti-Semitism for two thousand years. Actually, the statement is not a declaration of self-incrimination. It is a legal formula whereby the people take responsibility for the death of a criminal but rather than culpability it has to do with assuring justice is served. We have to remember the evangelist knows that Jesus was innocent. The crowd did not. Even more unfortunate is the fact that the Church promulgated this so-called indictment of the Jews by calling them the "Christ killers". Without its condemnation I doubt Hitler could have carried out his mass extermination of the Jewish people as successfully as he did.

That said, the Second Vatican Council clearly said that the Jews of Jesus' time, or any other time, were not guilty of Jesus' death. The fact is the Jews could not crucify anyone. If they truly wanted to kill Jesus they could have taken him outside the walls of the city and stoned him to death as they did St. Stephen. Only the Romans crucified people. No matter how many times Pontus Pilate washed his hands, he and the Roman government were responsible for Jesus' death.

Finally, only Matthew describes the actual resurrection, at least in part. In 28:2-4 he tells us there was a great earthquake and an angel came down from heaven and rolled back the stone. The guards that had been placed by the tomb apparently witnessed this.[41] The women seemed to have come to the tomb shortly afterwards. This is consistent with Matthew's style for just as the angel explained Jesus' birth he now explains his resurrection.

## MATTHEW'S RESURRECTION STORY (28:1-20)

Matthew adds one appearance of Jesus after he rose from the dead. There's always been some discussion as to whether the original copy of Mark contained a resurrection story and that it may have been lost. If this were the case then this narrative may not be originally from Matthew but most scholars believe it probably is. Contrary to the resurrection stories in Luke which all occur in and around Jerusalem, Matthew's appearance takes place in Galilee. This fulfills the words of the angel at the tomb when he tells the women, "Go tell my brothers to go to Galilee and there they will see me." (28:10) It is here Jesuse commissions the twelve to preach the Gospel to all nations and provides them with the formula to baptize in the name of the Trinity. These words reflect that Matthew's community was baptizing in the name of the Trinity whereas Acts 2:38 reflects the earlier custom of baptizing only in the name of Jesus. While this narrative sounds like Jesus is leaving them, there is no ascension. Jesus also echoes the name Emmanuel, first given in Matthew 1:23 when he says, "Behold I am with you always . . ." (Matt. 28:20).

---

[41]    There is some similarity to this found in the second century Gospel of Peter. An Egyptian monk found a fragment of this Gospel in 1886. This fragment describes the resurrection as following an earthquake, the stone rolling back and two angels who reach to the heavens accompanying Jesus, who reaches above the heavens, carrying his cross.

# MATTHEW'S JESUS

## Jesus the Divine?

As I mentioned above, Matthew presents Jesus as a New Moses but he is even more than Moses. While I don't believe that Matthew definitively claims Jesus is divine he definitely presents him as the glorified Lord. In the very beginning of the Gospel, the Magi "prostrated themselves before the baby Jesus and did him homage"(2:11). At the end of the Gospel the disciples worshipped him (28:17). During the temptation in the desert the devil asks Jesus to prostrate before him and Jesus responded that only God should be worshipped (4:10). All this may be a subtle way of introducing Jesus as divine and perhaps that's part of Matthew's agenda. For instance, Mark's use of "Son of God" refers to Jesus as a king who will rule the coming Kingdom of God. Matthew 11:27 presents Jesus as Son of God in a different way. Here Jesus says, "All things have been handed over to me by my Father and no one knows the Father except the Son and anyone who the Son wishes to reveal him." Matthew seems to be taking Jesus even a step further than Luke. While Luke presents him as greater than angels Matthew sees him as next to God. The later the date the Gospels are composed it seems the more divine Jesus becomes.

## Jesus and the Kingdom

For Matthew, the Kingdom of God is not something that is to arrive in the future. It is already here, manifested in the community of believers, i.e. the Church. His is the only Gospel where Jesus says, "You are Peter and upon the rock I will build my Church"(16:18). Jesus inaugurated it, he is its Lord and he will be with it always until the end of time (28:20).

## Israel's Messiah

Matthew's Jesus is definitely Israel's Messiah. The use of multiple references from the Hebrew Scriptures affirms this. He is the Son of David and the King of Israel. Matthew's Jesus says that he has devoted himself and his ministry exclusively "to the lost sheep of the house of Israel" (10: 5-6; 15:24). Unfortunately, the Jews, represented by Herod, the chief priests and the scribes, reject him. For Matthew, because of this, the Messiah of Israel is transformed into the Messiah for the world. "Go therefore and make disciples of all nations" (28:19).

## The Stoic and Authoritative Teacher

The Jesus we find in Matthew is rather austere and lacks emotion. He doesn't have the sensitivity and compassion that we find in the man described by Luke. Matthew's Jesus lacks the passion of Mark's Jesus. As in Mark, he is portrayed as a teacher but he is a teacher extraordinaire. He teaches with authority, meaning that he doesn't quote other Rabbis and then chooses the one he agrees with. Other Rabbis are never mentioned. Jesus' words have the authority of God. "You have heard the commandment, but I say unto you . . ." God gave the commandments to Moses. Jesus takes God's words and adds to them. Now that's speaking with authority!

While his teachings contain terse ethical and moral statements they are lumped into great discourses. Matthew's Jesus is quite wordy. Most scholars believe that Matthew added a lot of material to his sources. If you compare Luke's Sermon on the Plain with Matthew's Sermon on the Mount you'll find about 30 verses in Luke versus 102 verses in Matthew. It's quite obvious Matthew wants to portray Jesus as a preacher who teaches the community everything they need to know to stand up against the challenges of the Pharisees and the world. In the flesh Jesus preached to the Jews in Palestine. In the Spirit Jesus will now preach through his disciples to the world.

## Conclusion

Matthew presents Jesus as a new Moses who is far more than a man and far greater than a prophet. He is a person who not only speaks with divine authority but also has divine authority and, even more than that, he has such a unique relationship with the Father that he is the only one who knows the Father and the Father's plan for the world. He is so much greater than Moses, or anyone else, that both Jew and Gentile bow before him as if he were a god. He is Israel's Messiah but also the Son of God who has already ushered in the Kingdom of God manifested in and through the Church in which he will continue to be present forever.

# PERSONAL REFLECTION

Chapters five through seven in Matthew contain the well-known "Sermon on the Mount". The sermon includes the most demanding and comprehensive teaching in the entire New Testament and I could probably put together an entire book of reflections on its content. In this reflection, I am just going to focus on one thought, the idea that to be truly Christian we must go way above and beyond what society requires of us.

In the sermon Jesus tell us that while laws are good what really counts is what's in one's heart. In other words, what we think is just as compelling and pejorative as what we do. For example, it is unlawful to murder but Jesus tells me that if I am angry with my brother or sister I will be liable to judgment (5:21). In other words, if I dare to call myself a Christian, anger must be eliminated even from my thoughts. The same is true of lustful intentions, which for Jesus, is equivalent to adultery.

Retaliation is not permitted. In fact we are told to love our enemies and pray for our persecutors (5:39-46). Forgiveness is the mark of what it means to be a follower of Christ (6:14) and judging others brings God's Judgment on us (7:1-2). In addition to this, we must be so truthful in everything we do that no one will ask us to swear to what we say (5:33-37).

As I reflect on these unbelievably demanding commandments I can see how I fail to live them out on a day to day basis. For example, I may not judge others out loud but I certainly judge people in my thoughts. Sometimes I hold back my forgiveness and sadly I must admit that there are times when I think about revenge.

Many of us, even scripture scholars, question the authenticity of these sayings. Surely, Jesus can't expect us to be perfect. Yet he does say, "You must be perfect as your heavenly Father is perfect" (5:48). Quite frankly, I don't know anyone who is this holy or this good.

Still, I don't think Matthew's Jesus spoke these words idly. I don't think he put them out there simply as unattainable ideals. We can attain them and the answer as to how is also given in the Sermon. Jesus tells us in 6:25-34 that we need to trust in God in all things. We need to ask God for all things (7:7-11) and the one thing we need to ask for the most is the grace to live out these commands. We need the Holy Spirit to guide us along the way to right living and empower us to live as Jesus did.

It's a difficult and challenging task but it's one that everyone can meet if only we turn to God and honestly seek to do God's will.

# Chapter Four

# THE GOSPEL OF JOHN

The Gospel of John is very different than the other three Gospels. While it follows the general outline of Mark, which begins with John the Baptizer, followed by the ministry of Jesus, the conspiracy of the Jewish leaders, the crucifixion and death of Jesus and the empty tomb, only the *Feeding of the Multitude, Walking on Water* and the passion narrative are common to both John and the Synoptic Gospels. However, even these three instances are described from a different perspective. So it's safe to say the Gospel of John is derived from a completely different tradition than Matthew, Mark and Luke. It's even possible that the author of John was not even aware of the Synoptic Gospels.

The Gospel focuses on a ministry which took place primarily in Judea and actually, via the use of Jewish feast days, indicates it was at least two years long. The Synoptics relate a ministry of less than a year. They state that Jesus' ministry in Galilee began after the arrest of John the Baptist (Mark 1:14 et al). John tells us Jesus had a rather extensive baptism ministry and spent many days teaching and working signs in Jerusalem and its environs rather than just the final week of his life as the Synoptics indicate. Much of this took place before John the Baptist was arrested.

John contains fewer miracles, seven versus twenty five in the other three Gospels. He never uses the word, Church. Apostle is used only once in reference to The Twelve and there isn't a single parable. There is no institution of the Eucharist nor does Jesus seem to celebrate a ritual meal the night before he died. He does gather with his disciples for supper but in John it is not a Passover meal since John states that the night of Passover took place the day after Jesus died on the cross.

John's Gospel is not filled with terse sayings as in the Synoptics. Rather, John's Jesus gives us long discourses. Unlike Matthew, the discourses are not moral guides for right living but are used to explain who Jesus is and what is required for discipleship. Jesus' miracles are also greatly expanded and are used to reveal that Jesus is the revelation of God and that salvation comes through him. While a miracle described in Mark, for example, might contain only a few verses, some of the ones in John may contain over 40 verses. As I stated above, except for the *Miracle of the Loves* and the *Walking on Water* narratives, there are no other miracles John shares in common with any of the Synoptics.[42] John also contains different resurrection narratives, which apparently are described by two different authors and in completely different settings.

The Gospel of John is by far the most theological Gospel with a significant emphasis on the divinity of Jesus that is not found in the Synoptics. It is highly symbolic and literary and probably grew out of theological reflection which as we shall see, most likely developed in the particular community inhabited by the author and/or the Gospel's editors.

## WHO WROTE IT?

This is the only Gospel where the author is mentioned. However, rather than explicitly naming him, he is called the *Beloved Disciple* (BD). The identity of BD has been the subject of controversy for some time but most particularly in the twentieth century. Tradition tells us that John the son of Zebedee, one of the Twelve Apostles, was the beloved disciple, however, today many scholars disagree with that conclusion. The Sons of Zebedee are only mentioned once in Chapter 21, which was written by someone other than the original author and, in this case, they are not mentioned by name. The author is very familiar with the environs of the city of Jerusalem and also with Temple ritual and worship. It's highly unlikely that a Galilean fisherman would have had such knowledge.

---

[42] The healing of the cripple at the pool of Bethesda and the man born blind have parallels in the Synoptic Gospels but the circumstances and the settings are quite different which seems to indicate that the Evangelist or the redactors were following a different tradition.

Age comes into question as well. Even if John the Apostle was only in his late teens when Jesus called him, by the time the Gospel was written he would have been well into his eighties. As I mentioned above, most people of that time only lived till their mid-forties. While living into one's eighties was certainly not impossible it was highly improbable. Finally, the Sons of Zebedee in chapter 21 are differentiated from BD indicating to me that BD is not one of them.

I believe the identity of the author is cleverly portrayed in the text as Lazarus, the one whom Jesus raised from the dead. I am not alone in this conclusion but I am certainly in the minority which, quite frankly surprises me. My reasons are as follows:

1) Whoever wrote this Gospel was a Palestinian Jew who, as I said above, was very familiar with the city of Jerusalem and temple worship. Lazarus lived in Bethany, which was only about two miles from Jerusalem. After his death, during the period reserved for mourning, we are told that many of the Jews were there to comfort his sisters. *The Jews* is a title used by John, which I believe, mostly refers to the leaders of the Jewish people (more on this later). In other words, they were important people who came from Jerusalem. Lazarus had to be wealthy and important himself for them to be there. That Lazarus was wealthy is obvious from the text. John11:38 says that Lazarus was buried in a cave with a stone rolled across it. Such a tomb was reserved for the rich. His sister Mary anointed Jesus with spikenard, expensive oil, so expensive we are told in 12:5 it was worth three hundred days wages. The Gospel says that BD "was known to the High Priest" (18:15). Certainly, this could not have been a Galilean fisherman. The High Priest would only befriend someone who was at his level both socially and financially. Lazarus, likely, was such a person.

2) John 11:5 says that Jesus loved Lazarus and his sisters Martha and Mary. Aside from BD, this is the only passage in John that directly says Jesus loved anyone.[43] Furthermore, in 11:36 the Jews say, "See how he loved him."

---

[43]  There is only one instance in the other Gospels- the story of the rich man recorded by Mark. Mark 10:21 says "Jesus looking at him, loved him and said…" I've often wondered if this rich young man was Lazarus.

3) BD is not mentioned until after Lazarus is raised from the dead. It seems to me that the Lazarus story is the author's way of introducing BD.

4) When BD goes into the empty tomb (20:8) he "saw and believed". Peter on the other hand did not understand. Since BD had already died and was raised he would understand the surroundings in the tomb better than anyone else.

5) Chapter 21:20-23 describes a conversation between Jesus and Peter regarding BD. This chapter was clearly written by someone other than the Beloved Disciple. In fact, in verse 24 he states that he is not BD. The dialogue between Peter and Jesus implies that the community believed that BD would not die and were disturbed by the fact that he did die. It seems odd that they believed this person would not die unless, of course, he had already died! If Lazarus were raised from the dead it would seem logical that he would remain alive at least until Jesus returned in glory. Why would God allow him the die again?

I believe the evidence is clear. The Beloved Disciple is Lazarus, the brother of Martha and Mary. Why the author decided to present Lazarus in this way is not clear. However, perhaps the original evangelist never mentioned BD. He may have been introduced by an editor of the Gospel. As we shall see below, this Gospel was probably edited a few times. Perhaps this particular editor knew that Lazarus was known to the community as the Beloved Disciple and described him as such.

The submission of Lazarus as the identity of the Beloved Disciple is not without complications. BD was present at the last meal the disciples had with Jesus. He was the one who laid his head on Jesus' chest. He is clearly presented as being superior to Peter but he is not on the Synoptic Gospels' list of the Twelve Apostles.

However, Bethany was a place that Jesus often frequented. It was in Bethany that he visited with Martha and Mary (Lk10:38-42). Mark says he was anointed in the home of Simon the Leper in Bethany (Mark 14:3-9). His triumphal entry into Jerusalem began there (Luke 19:28-38). Matthew 21:19 tells us that Jesus left Jerusalem and lodged in Bethany. Lazarus was not only raised from the dead in Bethany but a feast was also held in his home shortly thereafter; a feast that Jesus attended. Apparently, Bethany was an important stop for Jesus. It may have even been his home base when he preached in Jerusalem. This would mean that Lazarus and his sisters played a very important role in the ministry of Jesus as did the Beloved Disciple.

Yet, it seems strange that, in spite of all this, other than John's narrative about the resurrection of Lazarus, we know nothing about him. Oddly, no other Gospel mentions him. We shall address this later when we discuss the resurrection of Lazarus in more detail.

## DATE OF COMPOSITION

Scholars now believe that the Gospel of John is the result of a series of redactions. While BD is credited as the source of this Gospel it likely was written by a school of disciples who were an integral part of the community in which BD either founded or lived. I say this because there are numerous stylistic differences. For instance, the Prologue (1:1-18) contains a number of words are not found anywhere else in the Gospel. It sounds like a hymn which may have been sung by BD's community and is an obvious addition to the original Gospel.

The geography and chronology are often out of sequence. For example in 3:22 we read that Jesus went to Judea but in 2:23 we are told he is already there. 6:1 implies that Jesus is in Galilee although at the end of Chapter 5 he is in Jerusalem. Often Jesus' discourses seem to end only to begin again with a repetitive discourse that has been theologically changed. For example in 14:31, Jesus says, "Come let us go." and then continues to give three more chapters of discourses before he finally leaves. Finally, the Gospel appears to end with 20:31 only to begin again with Chapter 21, which recounts more resurrection appearances in a different geographical location.

A possible scenario is that BD wrote the original Gospel between 65 and 75 **CE.** This document contained chapters 1-10, excluding the prologue and the discourses, plus a brief passion narrative. Sometime around 85 **CE,** this Gospel was edited either by BD or someone else. In this version, the miracles were re-written as "signs" and the cleansing of the Temple was moved from right before Jesus' arrest to Chapter 2. The resurrection of Lazarus was added, as well as some of the Last Supper discourses. In addition, the story of the crucifixion and death of Jesus was modified and some of the resurrection narratives were added. Finally around 95-100 **CE** or even later, the last chapter and the Prologue were added plus some modifications to the discourses of Jesus.

While all of this is pure hypothesis, it is one way to explain the many discrepancies cited above. Exactly how it happened will never be known.

# BACKGROUND

Since the Gospel of John is likely the result of several redactions that cover a span of about 30 years, the document must have circulated among several Christian communities or there were some dramatic Christological changes in one community over that period of time. Many Scholars feel that the original version of John was written in Palestine and then taken to Ephesus in Asia Minor. The earliest traditions place the origin of the Gospel, at least as we have it today, in Ephesus. The Christian community of Ephesus may have been founded by St. Paul who for a while made it his home base. However, the Gospel exhibits little Pauline teaching and what it does share with Paul is found in the disputed epistles. For example, the Prologue, 1:1-5, 10-11, strongly resembles Col. 1:15-20 where Jesus is described as pre-existent and through whom all things were created. John refers to Jesus as the "Lamb of God who takes away the sins of the world" and Jesus' death on the cross is placed in the context of the killing of the Passover lambs. In a similar way Paul's preaches that Jesus suffered and died for the sins of mankind. However, while Paul emphasizes the resurrection of Jesus as a fundamental belief, John focuses on the belief in Jesus as the Messiah and most particularly, the Son of God. Paul's emphasis is on salvation by faith rather than being justified by the LAW. In a way, John certainly focuses on believing but, contrary to Paul, belief in the words and deeds of Jesus act as a means to salvation (See John 6:19-47, 7:60-68, 15:24).[44]

John's high Christology and sophisticated theological thought indicates that the Gospel is of a later origin than the Synoptic Gospels and that he had a more sophisticated audience. Like the other Gospels, especially Matthew, he is addressing issues present in his community. What were those issues?

## Salvation Requires Baptism and the Spirit

One of the problems John faced had to do with the requirement for belonging to his community and hence being "saved" or put right with God. The dialogue between Nicodemus and Jesus indicates that unless one is born

---

[44]   Ironically, John never uses the word *faith*. However, he uses the word *believe* ninety eight times.

from above by water and the Holy Spirit one cannot belong to the community or obtain salvation. (3:1-8) Perhaps there were Jews in the community who said that circumcision or a simple profession of faith was sufficient for salvation. Others may have said that only the baptism of John was required.[45]

## The Docetic Heresy

Another problem was a heresy known as Docetism or at least a pre-Docetism. The Docetists were a second century philosophical group of Gentile Christians who believed that Jesus only appeared to have a physical body. In other words he was a phantasm. This stemmed from the belief that all material things including the human body were evil. As a result, Jesus could not have been human since God could not exist in an evil body. Hence, they believed that Jesus was only a divine spirit.

## The Ebionite Heresy

Another heretical group, which may have influenced John, was known as the Ebionites who believed that Jesus was not divine[46]. Rather he was a human being who was begotten by God at his baptism and, as a result, lived the Jewish law to perfection. They did not believe in the virginal conception or that Jesus died for the redemption of sin. Since their focus was on obedience to the Law of Moses they opposed St Paul's teaching and regarded him as a heretic. Most likely, Ebionite thought was not fully developed when John was written but, like Docetism, it was certainly emerging.

---

[45]  Acts 18:25 mentions Apollos, an Alexandrian Jew, who preached the Gospel of Jesus but only knew the baptism of John. It may be that John's Jesus is referring to this group of believers in his exchange with Nicodemus.

[46]  The Ebionites probably descended from the Jerusalem Church and reflected the early beliefs of this original group of the followers who were then known as "The Way" (Acts 9:2). They practiced the simple communistic lifestyle described in Acts 4:32-34, accepted only an Aramaic version of the Gospel of Matthew and rejected Paul's epistles. Like the early Church they looked forward to the return of Christ in glory to establish his kingdom.

John responded to these two sects in the prologue by clearly stating that Jesus was one with God, therefore divine, and that he was also human because "the Word became flesh" (1:14). Throughout the Gospel the Evangelist portrays Jesus as one with the Father who reveals God to the world. But he also shares meals with his disciples (13:2), washes their feet (13:4-12), insists that Thomas places his hands in his wounds (20:27) and is embraced by Mary Magdalene (20:17) demonstrating that he was a corporal being.

## The Jews

A group of people referred to as "The Jews" also influenced this Gospel. It's a strange phrase, especially when we find it on the lips of Jesus! Jesus, as a Jew, would never refer to his own people as "The Jews". In this Gospel, Jesus even refers to Jewish law as *their law* (15:25). The original Evangelist himself was probably Jewish so this title would certainly not have come from him. Often the title seems to refer to the Jewish leaders who opposed Jesus but this is not always the case.

Most likely, this title was inserted by one of the Gentile Christian editors and pertains to the Pharisees in the 90's **CE** who stood in opposition to BD's community of believers. As was the case in Matthew's community, the Pharisees had redefined Judaism after the destruction of the Temple and mounted strong opposition to the teachings of the Christians. I'm quite certain that this term reflects this conflict so I think it's fair to say that the phrase "The Jews" mostly refers to all those Jews who contested Christian teaching in the later part of the first century, particularly the teaching of BD's community. The term could also refer to Jewish Christians who seem to be struggling with the Johanine notion that Jesus was God and as a result were rejected by the author or the editors of this Gospel.

## The Samaritans

It seems likely that a large part of BD's community were Samaritans. Acts 8:4-40 indicates a fairly large missionary effort in Samaria. The story of the Samaritan woman (4:1-42) and the conversion of an entire Samaritan village probably reflect this. Some of these Samaritans likely had leadership roles and perhaps one of the editors was a Samaritan. The term "The Jews" is a phrase Samaritans would use to refer to the Jewish people especially leaders and other Jews who were antagonistic to them and their Christian brothers and sisters.

## The Essenes

Another group, which may have influenced this Gospel, at least literarily, is the Essenes. The writings of the Qumran community, believed to be of Essene origin, often use the terms light and darkness to reflect good and evil. John's prologue (1:5) as well as 8:12 reflects this usage.

Some believe that John the Baptizer was an Essene and, if so, some of his disciples were probably Essenes as well. Since some of John's disciples became disciples of Jesus, their thought and background may be reflected in this Gospel.[47]

All this, of course is based on supposition, however, the evidence strongly implies that BD's community was fragmented by a diversity of beliefs regarding the nature of Jesus and his mission. The authors are determined to set the record straight and clearly state that Jesus is the revelation of God in the flesh. Belief in Jesus is the key to salvation. In fact, he is the only means to salvation. According to John, any deviation from this is clearly false teaching.

---

[47] It's certainly possible that Jesus may have been an Essene as well. Their apocalyptic view is similar to that of Mark's Jesus. Like Jesus, they opposed divorce and most were celibate. Like the early Christian community they shared everything in common, used baptismal rituals for initiation and participated in solemn meals, one of which included bread and wine. However, they were also somewhat different, Unlike Jesus, they were very anti-Temple and strongly maintained ethical and ritual purity. Still, Jesus had to learn how to read and understand the Scripture somewhere. Most likely, his parents were illiterate and a local Rabbi could never have given Jesus his vast understanding of Scripture. Of all the Jewish sects in the first century, aside from the Scribes in Jerusalem and some of the Pharisees, no one except the Essene community at Qumran was capable of educating Jesus at the level we read about in the Gospels. While we will probably never know how Jesus was educated, the Essene community at Qumran is an option to be considered.

## The Role of Prophecy

In many ways the Gospel of John is so different from the Synoptic Gospels that often its authenticity as an accurate presentation of the words and deeds of Jesus is questioned. How can John present Jesus as divine when the Synoptics, especially Mark, portray him as very human? How could the writers remember the long discourses and record them with such detail? In the past, many scholars dismissed the historicity of John; however, recent archeological discoveries indicate that, at least the original author provides very accurate descriptions of the environs in and around Jerusalem. So the question that still must be asked is, "Can we reconcile the fourth Gospel with the other three?" The answer is "yes" and "no".

A way to describe the four Gospels is that the three Synoptic Gospels mainly present Jesus in the flesh where-as the fourth Gospel portrays Jesus as the risen Lord. Hence, the first three are more biographical while the Gospel of John is more of a description of the risen Jesus who is present in the Christian community through the Holy Spirit—hence more spiritual.[48]

The role of prophecy was very important the early Church. Paul tells us in 1 Corinthians that first there are apostles, second there are prophets, third there are teachers, etc.(12:28). So, next to apostles, prophets had the most important role in the community. The believers felt that God spoke through these prophets. They were literally possessed by the Holy Spirit. The Holy Spirit was believed to be the Spirit of Jesus (Acts 5:9). It was through the Holy Spirit that Jesus continued to be present in the community. When the Spirit spoke through a prophet the community believed that Jesus was speaking to them. Prophets advised and guided the believers in the ways of the faith. When new issues arose which hadn't been addressed by Jesus in the flesh the Church turned toward it's prophets to provide it with answers. Since the Holy Spirit spoke for Jesus, they believed Jesus continued to teach them.

---

[48]  Clement of Alexandria (ca. 200 CE) wrote, as quoted by Eusebius in his Ecclesiastical History, "John, last of all the evangelists, being conscious that the corpus (events in the ministry of Jesus) had been made clear in the (other three) Gospels, was encouraged by those who knew him, and being divinely inspired by the Spirit, composed a *spiritual Gospel*." (italics mine) This basically says that Clement believed that the Gospel of John was not historical.

St Paul states in Galatians 1:11-12 that the Gospel he preaches is not of human origin. "For I did not receive it from any human being, nor was I taught it, but it came through a revelation from Jesus Christ." The Jesus he is speaking of was not the Jesus in the flesh but the risen Christ who manifested himself to Paul and the community via visions and prophecies.

John 14:26 also provides us with a clue to the source of his Gospel: "The Advocate, the Holy Spirit that the Father will send in my name—he will teach you everything and remind you of all that I told you." Here, John's Jesus is clearly telling his disciples that he will continue to communicate with them through the Holy Spirit.

Consequently, I believe most of the discourses found in John, were not spoken by Jesus in the flesh. Rather, they are a summary of the teachings that Jesus gave to John's community through its prophets. This revelation was provided over a period of time as issues arose and the situation in the community changed. Over that period of time it was either written down or became part of the community's oral tradition.

One of the main reasons that I believe this to be the case is that Jesus in the flesh could never have told his disciples or any other Jew that he was God or that he was the revelation of God. The Jewish belief in one God was so entrenched in their minds that everyone would have deserted him. Most likely, they would have stoned him to death. Remember, they stoned Stephen for a far lesser offence.

John's Gospel is a continuing series of confrontations between Jesus and the Jewish leaders. As I said above, these leaders were not the religious leaders who were contemporary with Jesus in the flesh. They were the Pharisees and other Jews who opposed John's Jesus and his community in the 90's **CE**. John's Jesus was the risen Jesus who continued to be present through the power of the Spirit.

As a result, even though John doesn't provide the words of Jesus in the flesh, those words are still inspired since they were still spoken by Jesus, albeit the risen Jesus, speaking through the Holy Spirit.


## THE BEGINNING

The Prologue (1:1-18)

As I stated above, John's Prologue (1:1-14) was a later addition to the original Gospel. It may have been added by an early editor or by the same person who added the Epilogue (21:1-25). Part of the Prologue was probably an edited form of a hymn that was sung by the community and like the infancy narratives of Luke and Matthew serves as a preview of the basic themes of the Gospel. These themes include the Word who is pre-existent. This Word is life and light in the context of the Essene concept of light versus darkness. The Word is the truth which sets us free. It clearly identifies the Word (*logos* in the Greek) as Jesus Christ. Since the Word is pre-existent, Jesus the Christ is also pre-existent. However, not only is Christ the Word, but this Word is creative and so, Christ, as the Word of God, is also the Creator God. It's obvious that the hymn parallels Chapter One of Genesis. As the spirit of the Lord moved over the waters and spoke, things came to be. According to John, the one who spoke in the beginning was the *logos*. The word *logos* implies wisdom so the prologue is basically telling us that Jesus imparts to the world wisdom, not human wisdom, but God's wisdom.

Later in the hymn we are told that this word, this wisdom, becomes flesh and literally in the Greek, "pitched his tent among us" (1:14). So the sacred author is telling us that Jesus is a human being who is also the Word/Wisdom of God that reveals God to us. "Whoever has seen me has seen the Father." (14:8). For John, Jesus is portrayed as a sage but he is unlike any other sage because his words are literally God's words.

Notice the break from verses 6 to 9. This is not a part of the hymn. The author inserts this to be sure that the reader understands that John the Baptizer is inferior to Jesus. As we saw in Luke it seems apparent that there was a significant group of people who believed that John the Baptizer was the Messiah or perhaps that John was greater than Jesus. The Evangelist, like Luke, makes sure that his audience understands that he is only the messenger. He reinforces this theme later on in this chapter where-in the Baptist himself confirms this (1:21).

1:11 reflects the conflict between the leaders of the Jews and the members of BD's community. As Matthew portrays the rejection of the Christians by the Jews through Herod, John makes essentially the same statement in 1:11 but much more directly, "He came to what was his own but his own people did not accept him"

There is another break in the hymn in 1:12-13 which is used to introduce his thesis that salvation comes from accepting Jesus. It is not because of anything we do; it has nothing to do with what race we are born into. It is God's doing. As Jesus tells Nicodemus, those who believe in him are reborn from above. (3:3)

The prologue ends with verse 18, "No one has ever seen God. The only Son of God, who is at the Father's side, has revealed him."[49] The phrase differentiates the Word of God from God. In other words, in some mysterious way Jesus, even though he is the Word "who is with God and was God" he is not God; he is the son of God. Until the doctrines of the Trinity and the dual nature of Jesus were adopted, Church Fathers would be discussing this confusing statement for 300 years.

## The First Disciples (1:35-51)

John is the only Gospel which tells us that some of the apostles were disciples of John the Baptizer. Their call seems to be different than the Synoptic version. For example, in Matthew, Mark and Luke, Jesus calls Peter and Andrew while they are mending their nets by the Sea of Galilee (Matt 14:18-22 et al). John tells us that Andrew is a disciple of John the Baptizer and JB tells him and others to follow Jesus. Andrew in turn gets his brother Peter who seems to be nearby (also a disciple of John?) to come and meet Jesus. Phillip and Nathanael are also among those called but John never gives us a list of the Twelve Apostles. In fact, he only refers to the Twelve one time (6:70). In all other instances they are referred to as the disciples which often include more than the Twelve.

## THE BOOK OF SIGNS (1:19-12:50)

Scholars call 1:19-12:50 the Book of Signs. It actually begins before Jesus' first encounter with John the Baptizer's disciples. This part of the Gospel will

---

[49]   This translation is mine. The RSV reads…the only son who is in the bosom of the Father, has made him known. The NAB reads … The only Son, God, who is at the Father's side, has revealed him. The New Jerusalem Bible says… "it is the only Son, who is nearest the Father's heart, who has made him known." The literal translation, which I have used, strongly implies that there are two gods, the Father and Jesus. Jesus is begotten of God, therefore separate from God but is still divine- a concept that is easy for the Gentiles to accept and impossible for the Jews. No one seems to be sure of exactly what the Evangelist meant to say here. In most every case the translators have glossed the text to reflect current theology.

serve to show who Jesus is and except for "The Jews "there are many kinds of people who believe in him. In this section Jesus engages people with extended conversations or dialogues and at times performs miracles which the evangelist calls signs. In each event, Jesus reveals himself to his listeners and many of them recognize and accept him as the Messiah and the Son of God.

As we shall see, the evangelist uses a literally device, called "Johanine Misunderstanding". It involves a play on words, figurative language or metaphors, wherein a specific word or saying has more than one meaning. At first, the listener misunderstands Jesus who then repeats himself but in a different way to help the listener understand. This allows John's Jesus to explain his teachings more fully and also demonstrate how one gradually comes to belief in Jesus.

There are seven signs, the number seven indicating perfection or completeness. All of them are miracles, but there is some controversy as to what should be included in the seven. Some omit the walking on the water pericope for a couple of reasons. First, it is very short and unlike the others doesn't seem to teach much of anything. Second, the text found in 6:19, which is usually translated "they saw Jesus walking on the sea" could also be translated "on the seashore" or "by the sea" which would mean this is not a miracle. Those who omit this text say that the seventh sign is the resurrection. I tend to agree with this because, except for the "Walking on Water" story, each sign seems to be greater than the one that precedes it. The raising of Lazarus can only be topped by the resurrection of Jesus, the ultimate and final sign that he is indeed the Son of God. However, I would include the entire paschal event as the seventh sign. John's Jesus reigns from the cross. As the serpent was lift up by Moses so too Jesus is lifted up on the cross and subsequently raised to a new and everlasting life as a sign that he has overcome death.

As I said above, a series of long discourses are intermingled with the signs. They begin with Nicodemus (3:1-21) followed by the meeting with the Samaritan woman (4:4-42). Also included within this book are: the Bread of Life discourse (6:22-59), the dialogue with the "The Jews" regarding Moses and the Messiah (7:14-31, 40-52), Jesus and Abraham (8:31-59) and The Good Shepherd (10:1-21). In between these there are also some very short discourses which I will not address. Again, these discourses, like the seven signs, are meant to reveal who Jesus is but they also reveal some theology that appears to be uniquely Johanine. Moreover, they indicate that there is a great deal of hostility between the leaders of the Jews and Jesus. This probably represents the antagonism between the community of the Beloved Disciple and the synagogue Jews of the 90's **CE**.

## The First Sign—The Wedding at Cana (2:1-12)

The story of the wedding at Cana is the first sign. Cana, a small village near Nazareth, is mentioned only in John's Gospel. Notice that Jesus' mother and brothers are in attendance. Oddly, the evangelist never tells us the name of Jesus' mother. In addition, Jesus addresses his mother in a very strange way. He calls her "woman", *gounai* in Greek, which is literally translated "Madam". He refers to her in the same way while on the cross (19:26). While it is a normal polite form of address, outside the Gospel, there is no attestation of this word ever being used in reference to one's mother. In addition, Jesus response seems to have a hostile tone, " . . . how does that concern affect me?" Literally it reads, "What is this to me and to you?" Perhaps Jesus is a bit perturbed because his "hour has not yet come", *hour* meaning his passion, death and resurrection. Perhaps he doesn't think it's wise to use his power to resolve a family matter. On the other hand, his mother may be symbol of someone or something else.

I say this because John uses the word *gounai* in only three other places. He addresses the woman at the well in this way as well as the adulterous woman and Mary Magdalene. In all three instances, the women are of questionable reputation. Why would John's Jesus address his own mother in the same way? Perhaps BD or one of the editors is not literally referring to the mother of Jesus at all. Perhaps he is referring to the Church, i.e. his community. In the first epistle of John, the same author refers to his Church as "chosen Lady"(1 John 1:1). On the Cross Jesus gives the Beloved Disciple custody of his mother.[50] Could this mean custody of BD's community? His Church is certainly sinful, demanding and errant in its ways and this may be the editor's way of giving authority to the Beloved Disciple over his divided community.

The six stone jars contain water that is normally used for ceremonial washings[51]. The use of this water for something other than ritual purification

---

[50] It's extremely doubtful that Mary or any other women were at the foot of the cross. Both the Jews and the Romans demanded that women be kept at quite a distance from the victims. This reinforces the notion that Jesus' mother is used symbolically by John.

[51] Ritual washings were common among the Jews and prescribed in the Book of Leviticus. They were very serious rites. Often they were accompanied by sacrificial offerings of animals or grain. Such washings were required of a woman after her period or after childbirth; for anyone who came in contact

indicates that in this new covenant, which is being ushered in by Jesus, ritual or ceremonial washings are no longer required. These will be replaced by the new wine, wine which is far better than the wine of the Old Covenant. This wine comes from Jesus himself. It represents the wisdom and revelation that only Jesus can give. It is more rich and plentiful than all the previous wisdom and revelation combined.[52]

In essence, I believe this is what the story is really about. It is an allegory wherein Jesus' mother represents the Church, the servants are the ministers or Deacons of the Church, the Chief Steward is the Bishop or Presbyter of the Church; the water symbolizes baptism and the wine the Holy Spirit. The old covenant represented by the six stone jars is being replaced by the new and everlasting covenant. The wine in its abundance represents this new way, the Kingdom of Heaven, which is being ushered in by Jesus. Matthew's Jesus tells us that "you cannot put new wine into old wineskins" (Matt 9:17) meaning that the new covenant cannot be contained with the limits of the Law of Moses. At the last supper, Jesus gives his disciples the cup of wine and says, "This is the cup of the new covenant . . ." (Luke 22:20). As with all of John's signs, this narrative points to something much deeper. It speaks to the Church of the Beloved Disciple telling its ministers and leaders to do what Jesus tells them. They must listen to him because he is the one who has ushered in the Kingdom of God and it is the way of this Kingdom that must be followed. The old way was marked by ritual washings; the new way is marked by baptism and the presence of the Holy Spirit.

---

with anything deemed ritually impure, for example a corpse, or even a sacred object. Any contact with blood required a ritual bath. A soldier who came back from a "Holy War" had to go through a seven day purification. In all these situations the person involved was thought to be unclean and therefore must be made presentable before the Lord.

[52]   A major theme in this Gospel is "replacement". Here we see Jesus replacing the Old Covenant with the New Covenant. Throughout the Gospel Jesus appears to replace everything Jewish. He replaces the Temple (2:13-22) Jewish feast days, especially Hanukah (10:22-30), Tabernacles (7:1-31) and Passover (6:31-40, 19:14). He replaces Moses and the LAW(5:45-47;6:32-33) as well as Abraham (8:31-59). For John, the "New Age" is upon us; the "Old Age" has passed away- replaced by Jesus and his word.

Notice that Jesus' mother accompanies him and his disciples to Capernaum but we never see her again until the scene at the foot of the cross.

## Nicodemus (3:1-21)

John tells us that Nicodemus is a Pharisee and a ruler of the Jews which means that he probably was a member of the Sanhedrin which was the governing body of the Jewish people. Jesus was brought before the Sanhedrin when he was tried.

Nicodemus comes to see Jesus at night which could mean he wanted to keep the meeting secret or it's simply John's way of using light and darkness to indicate that Nicodemus was not a true believer and therefore is still in darkness. He does attest to the fact that Jesus is a teacher who is from God because of the signs he is doing. He doesn't really ask Jesus a question but Jesus responds as though he had asked a question. He tells Nicodemus that if he wants to see the Kingdom of God he must be reborn. Nicodemus misunderstands and thinks that Jesus is referring to some form of re-incarnation. Jesus responds by rephrasing his answer.

As I mentioned above, this is a literary device called Johanine misunderstanding and we will see it often in this Gospel. The author uses a word that has multiple meanings. The responder misunderstands the word and Jesus repeats the answer in a different way, which allows him to more fully explain what he means. In this case the word in Greek is *anothen* which can mean "again" or "from above".[53]

Nicodemus thinks Jesus is talking about being reborn in the flesh but Jesus is really talking about the Spirit which is different since "flesh begets flesh and the spirit begets spirit" (3:6). To be reborn of water and the Spirit means that the true believer is baptized and when he is baptized the Holy Spirit dwells in him. This has nothing to do with who bore us or raised us; in other words social status and wealth, all products of the flesh, have nothing to do with being a child of God.

---

[53]   The New American Bible translation doesn't capture the difference. The Revised Standard Version (RSV) does. The RSV translates 3:3 as, "Truly I say to you, unless one is *born again*, he cannot see the Kingdom of God" (italics mine) hence leading to the misunderstanding by Nicodemus.

As I mentioned above, this exchange could also be a polemic against the followers of John the Baptist who had accepted Jesus as the Messiah but maintained a fundamental belief in the efficacy of John's baptism.

3:15-21 summarizes the basic message of John's Gospel: Jesus is the incarnation of God who has saved the world from condemnation by his death. Those who believe in him will have eternal life and those who don't will be condemned.[54] John 3:16, is probably the most popularized verse in Scripture. We see it on posters in football fields, baseball stadiums, basketball courts and hockey arenas to name a few. Basically, it provides God's motive for God's plan of salvation. It is simply because God loves us.

## The Woman at the Well (4:4-42)

On his way from Jerusalem to Galilee Jesus passes through Samaria. It is an unusual route since Jews avoided Samarians, so much so, that they would not pass each other on the same side of the street.[55] In John 8:46, the leaders accuse Jesus of being a Samaritan. This may stem from the fact that

---

[54]   Many fundamentalist Christians use this text as proof that the only people who can be "saved" are those who confess Jesus as their Lord and Savior. The Catholic Church, of which I am most familiar, differs with this judgment. The *Dogmatic Constitution on the Church* from the Second Vatican Council states, "Eternal salvation is open to those who, through no fault of their own, do not know Christ and his Church but seek God with a sincere heart, and under the inspiration of grace try in their lives to do his will, made known to them by the dictates of their conscience. Nor does Divine Providence deny the aids necessary for salvation to those who, without blame on their part, have not yet reached an explicit belief in God but strive to lead a good life, under the influence of God's grace." (DCC, Number 16)

[55]   This hatred stems from the fact that the Samaritans were Jews who mixed the cult of Yahweh with the various pagan cults introduced by the Assyrians when they conquered the Northern Kingdom, Israel in the eight century BCE. After the Jews returned from the Babylonian Captivity in the sixth century BCE the Samaritans tried to prevent them from rebuilding the Temple. The Samaritans, in turn, built a Temple on Mt Gerizim which the Jews destroyed. Consequently, they viewed each other as heretics and enemies.

he and his disciples traveled through Samaria or more likely because many of the believers in John's community were Samaritans.

The Samaritan woman is surprised that Jesus speaks to her, not only because she is a Samaritan but also because she is a woman. Generally, a woman who was alone was often deemed a prostitute. If a man engaged her in conversation it was usually to solicit her services. That's probably why the disciples, when they returned were amazed, not that he was talking to a Samaritan, but to a woman. It may also be why they didn't question him (4:27).

This encounter results in another discourse and the thrust of this story is about how one encounters Jesus and slowly comes to believe in him. We also have another example of Johanine misunderstanding. When Jesus tells her that he can give her living water she thinks that he is going to give her a drink from the well. Jesus then has the opportunity to explain himself more fully. He tells her that the water he has to give is the water that provides eternal life. Symbolically, this water represents the Holy Spirit. She still doesn't understand but she has become very interested and seeks to know more—the first sign of an emerging faith.

Jesus then brings up her past which is quite sordid and because he knows it she now believes that he is a prophet, again indicating that her faith is growing. Finally Jesus confronts her, telling her that he is the Messiah. In typical Johanine style she now has to believe it or reject it.

Part of this narrative (4:17-24) has to do with true worship. Here Jesus tells the woman that his followers do not worship God on a mountain or in a temple. True worship takes place in the heart and in the presence of the Holy Spirit where we recognize Jesus as the Son of God. One can say that it is through the Spirit that we behold the Son, the Truth, who is the splendor of God's glory and who leads us to worship the Father.

At this point the disciples interrupt the meeting and the woman returns to her town and tells everyone that she has met the Messiah, an indication that she has become a believer. Finally, because of her witness, the whole town goes out to meet Jesus and they become believers as well.

Acts 8:14 tells us that Samaria had accepted the Gospel and this story may have come from there. It's interesting that the woman, once she became a believer, became an apostle. The town believed because of her testimony (4:39). It's ironic that in this very patriarchal culture John would portray a woman being responsible for the conversion of many to the faith. As we shall see later other women play a prominent role in this Gospel.

Finally, John may be using this story to rebuff the Jews who are antagonistic to his community. He's saying that the Samaritans quickly came to believe in Jesus, whereas the Jews from Jerusalem, refused to believe. This idea of the Jerusalem leaders rejecting Jesus will continue as a common theme throughout this Gospel.

## The Second Sign—The Royal Official's Son (4:46-54)

The healing of the Royal Official's son is the second sign. It introduces a new theme, that Jesus' word is life-giving. This story is similar to the healing of the Centurion's Servant (Matt 8:5-13; Luke7:1-10). The Synoptic's version contrasts the faith of the Israelites with that of the Centurion, a Gentile. It's surprising that John doesn't do that. The royal official in John's story may be a Jew or a Gentile. No distinction is made. Jesus chides the Official after he makes his request to heal his son, saying that "Unless you people see signs and wonders you will not believe." (4:48). The Official came to Jesus believing he could cure his son and he trusted Jesus' promise that his son would live before he saw the sign/miracle. Still, he and his household only came to fully believe after he was certain about the timing of the miracle. The message here is twofold: 1) faith in Jesus can be life-giving to both the believer and his family and 2) if Jesus can bring someone near death back to life he will also provide eternal life for those who believe in him.

## The Third Sign—The Cure of the Paralytic on the Sabbath (5:1-18)

This incident intertwines a number of issues and sets the stage for a long discourse between Jesus and the leaders of the Jews. It takes place at a place described as "Sheep Gate" where there was a pool. Recently a pool with five porticos was discovered near the northeast wall of the Temple area. The place is called *Bethesda* in Aramaic and it is mentioned in the Qumran copper scroll.

Apparently there was a legend that the angel of the Lord came down upon the pool and stirred up the waters. If one would go into the pool at this precise time healings would take place. The man could not get into the pool because he was crippled and he had no one to help him.

Jesus cures him with a word telling him to stand up, pick up the mat he was lying on and walk. This leads to a major issue. It is the Sabbath and no one is allowed to carry anything on the Sabbath because it constitutes work. When the man is questioned by the authorities he tells them that he does not know who the man is that healed him but after a second encounter with Jesus he tells the authorities that it was Jesus. This leads to a confrontation with the leaders of the Jews who are infuriated because they feel that Jesus is making himself equal to God.[56]

All this opens the door for John's Jesus to give a detailed explanation of who he is and how he relates to his Father; how God reveals himself through his son and how God relates to the world. Jesus is like God because he too raises the dead and cures the sick. Jesus is so close to the Father that anyone who honors Jesus honors God; likewise anyone who offends him offends God. In fact, Jesus is so intimately united to God that he can do nothing on his own. His words are God's words, his actions God's actions. Jesus has been appointed to reveal God to the world—a key theme in John—and also to judge the world.

Jesus further tells his listeners that his witness is far greater that John the Baptist which is another polemic against the followers of JB. Yet, while his testimony is greater than John's because it comes directly from God, John's testimony regarding Jesus was indeed true. It is an indictment of the leaders of the Jews because they did not believe John and now they don't believe in Jesus. They searched the Scriptures for answers, which was a good thing, but not when there is someone before them through whom God is directly speaking.

## The Fourth Sign—The Multiplication of the Loaves (6:1-15)

This is the only miracle that is common to all four Gospels. John's version differs from the other three. Philip and Andrew are mentioned by

---

[56]  It was a general belief that, when God rested from his creative actions on the Sabbath, he continued the rule his creation and pass judgment upon it. After all, babies are born on the Sabbath, people die on the Sabbath, all other things continue their existence and so on. Jesus is saying that since he is doing the work of his Father he too can work on the Sabbath. This is an oblique way of saying that he is equal to God thus angering the Jews.

name as those who question Jesus regarding how to feed all the people. The crowd acknowledges that because of what Jesus has done he must be "The Prophet".[57] Finally, the story is described as taking place near the Feast of Passover. This last detail puts the story in a Eucharistic context and sets the stage for the discourse which follows.

Ironically, unlike the Synoptic versions Jesus himself distributes the bread and the fish. Perhaps, since there is no institution of the Eucharist in John, this action by Jesus reflects the distribution of the bread and wine by Jesus at the Last Supper.

## The Bread of Life Discourse (6:22-71)

This very long discourse reveals Jesus' primary role on earth and a new understanding regarding the Eucharistic bread and wine. Here Jesus distinguishes himself from Moses indicating that he is far greater than Moses. Moses' actions were not from Moses but from God. Since Jesus is divine his actions are God's actions because he has come from the Father and is united to the Father. Unlike the manna in the desert, Jesus is the true bread come down from heaven. He is the "Bread of Life" who feeds us and gives us everything we need.

There is a twofold meaning in these words. The term "Bread from Heaven" was a colloquial phrase for the revelation of God. Since the Jews believed that the Torah, i.e. the first five books of the Bible, more or less came directly from God they were referred to as "The bread come down from heaven". Now John's Jesus is saying that he is the bread come down from heaven meaning that he is the revelation of God. God sent him to earth to tell the world about the Father and to reveal the Son who was sent by the Father.

Then John's Jesus contrasts the manna in the desert with the bread he has to give. The Jews ate the manna and died but those who eat Jesus' bread will live forever. Then he drops the bomb so to speak. The bread that he is speaking of is his flesh and blood. We know that it is not his actual flesh

---

57  Notice the text says, "The Prophet" as opposed to "a prophet". Apparently there was a belief that a prophet like Moses, only greater, would return to Israel and perform signs and wonders as Moses did. Whether he was to be the Messiah or a different person is not known.

and blood but the Eucharistic bread and wine which sacramentally become his body and blood.

This is a new and difficult teaching for those of Jewish descent. According to the Law of Moses, to drink blood of any kind was an abomination and a grave sin. To drink human blood was cannibalistic and evil.

Prior the John's time, the Eucharist was most likely seen as a meal of remembrance that recalled Jesus' suffering and death. Initially, it may have been celebrated only once a year during Passover. Gradually, it became a Sunday celebration. In Paul's communities it was added to the end of the "Love Feast" which was a large fellowship meal (See 1 Cor. 11:17-34). It prefigured the great Messianic banquet which would take place when Jesus returned and established his Kingdom. While the bread and wine were seen as sacred, until the latter part of the first century, it's doubtful that anyone believed that the bread and wine became Jesus' flesh and blood. But here Jesus is actually talking about using the Eucharistic bread and wine for nourishment, not for the body but for the soul. This is truly spiritual food of which one must partake of to gain everlasting life.

As usual, Jesus' audience misunderstands him. They don't relate it to Eucharist and think he is speaking of the actual blood that is flowing through his veins. Many, we are told, left him and "returned to their former way" (6:66). John demonstrates Peter's loyalty and reiterates his theme of salvation through Jesus, when he says, "Master, to whom shall we go?" You have the words of eternal life." (6:68)

However, the words of 6:54 can be taken symbolically as well. The word that is used here for "eat" literally means to gnaw or chew on like an animal would chew on a bone. When we hear something profound and something that is difficult to understand we often say, "I need to chew on that for a while". Perhaps Jesus understands that, because this teaching is so different and difficult to digest, so to speak, one needs to think about it and pray about it for a while before he is able to accept it. This was not an easy teaching. Rather it was one that required meditation and prayer before one could come to understand that it concerned the mystery of the Eucharist.[58]

---

[58]   Another way to interpret these passages is solely in the context of Jesus as the revelation of God, i.e. the "bread come down from heaven". By using this colloquial term John's Jesus is basically saying he is the fulfillment of the Hebrew Scriptures, in a sense the replacement of those Scriptures because he tells us what the Father tells him. Metaphorically, he is the sacred scroll on

## More Debates with the Jews (7:1-8:59)

Chapter seven opens with a strange and disjointed narrative wherein Jesus tells his brothers that he is not going to the Feast of Tabernacles[59] in Jerusalem but then later goes to the feast in secret. His brothers try to get him to go to Jerusalem so that his disciples can see firsthand the signs he is doing yet, in previous chapters, Jesus has already worked many signs in Jerusalem. We are told the Jews in Jerusalem are trying to kill him yet his brothers want him to go there. Do they want him killed? John makes it a point to inform the readers that Jesus' brothers did not believe in him.

Acts tells us that his mother and his brothers became a part of the Jerusalem Church and James, the eldest brother, was the head of that Church until he was martyred in about 62 **CE.** The Jerusalem Church was primarily Jewish with a low Christology. Perhaps members of this Church were part of the Johanine community and this was John's way of saying that their belief that Jesus was not divine was erroneous. In other words, his brothers' disbelief was not that Jesus wasn't the Messiah; rather it was that he was not divine.

Jesus goes to the festival and the focus of the next two chapters is Jesus' continuing conflict with "The Jews" and the Pharisees. Chapter 7 highlights the evangelist's theme that Jesus has come from God and that, when he speaks, God is essentially speaking. As in "The Bread of Life" discourse he is compared with Moses (7:22-24). However, contrary to 6:66 where many of his followers left him, we are told in 7:31, "many in the crowd came to believe in him". From this point on the crowds, in general, become more

---

which the Word of God is written and we must eat this "scroll" if we are to truly understand and proclaim this new revelation. In Ezekiel 3:1-4, God tells Ezekiel to eat the sacred scroll so that he will be able to proclaim God's word to God's people. Eating the scroll symbolically means that Ezekiel has digested the Word of God. It has become a part of his very being such that he is now equipped to properly and boldly speak God's word. Those who believe in Jesus must chew on his words; allow them to become a part of their being so that they, like Ezekiel, can proclaim this Word to the world.

59    The Feast of Tabernacles or Booths was a harvest feast that took place in the fall. The Hebrew name is Succoth and it lasted for several days. Tabernacles celebrated God's gifts of rain, symbolized by pouring water from the pool of Siloam on the altar in the Temple, and sunlight, symbolized by the four torches that burned in the Court of the Women.

sympathetic to Jesus and his following increases and culminates with the resurrection of Lazarus.

The conflict continues, still somewhat disjointed, wherein Jesus is again portrayed as the source of life-giving water which, we are told, represents the Holy Spirit who will come after he is raised from the dead (7:37-39).

After the brief interruption with the pericope about the woman caught in adultery, the conflict continues through Chapter 8. Here Jesus is portrayed as the light of the world, another key theme presented in the prologue.[60] As in the prologue, the light is contrasted with the darkness which, of course, represents good versus evil. 8:21-30 tells us that Jesus needs no one else to support his testimony because he comes from God and he says only what the father tells him. In other words, God is his witness; he needs no other witness to authenticate his claims. The basic and essential claim at this point is that those who listen to him will be given everlasting life—literally "will not die" (8:24). They will understand this when he is "lifted up" (8:27) which either means when he is lifted up on the cross or raised from the dead. Notice again, how "many came to believe in him" (8:30).

8:31 marks a transition from the "Jews" who are antagonists to "those Jews who believe in him", probably the ones mentioned in 8:30. As I mentioned above these people most likely are the Jewish Christians who perhaps came from Jerusalem and who are now part of the Beloved Disciple's community in the 90s **CE.** They are those who still go to the synagogue but refuse to denounce Jesus because they don't want to be expelled from the synagogue. They are, in John's eyes, half-hearted Christians who refuse to make the leap of faith needed to fully belong the Christian community.

There is obvious tension here which reflects the conflict between BD's community and this group of Jewish Christians. Their problem is they can't accept the community's belief that Jesus is divine. This stumbling block probably led to the separation of the Jews and Gentiles in this community.

Instead of Moses, this crowd appeals to Abraham as if to resort to a higher authority. The basis of their argument is that since they are the children of

---

[60]   Some scholars believe that John's Jesus replaces the principle Jewish Feasts of Passover, Tabernacles and Succoth. An example is found in the discourses found in Chapters 7 and 8 with respect to the Feast of Tabernacles. Here Jesus is the life-giving water and he is the light of the world which replaces the water and the light celebrated during the feast. In the same way Jesus replaces Passover because he is the Bread of Life and the Lamb of God. More on this later.

Abraham they are God's chosen people and that's sufficient for salvation. Jesus tells them that salvation doesn't come from one's family tree but by doing the will of God. Since Jesus comes from God and speaks for God, salvation comes from doing his will.[61]

## The Adulterous Woman (8:1-11)

This particular story is not found in the earliest manuscripts and is a later insert which breaks up the discourses found in Chapters 7 and 8. It is found in most of the old Latin manuscripts and, as a result, only the Roman Catholic Church accepts the story as scripturally canonical.

Actually, the style and motifs are Lucan and, in fact, the story is found in some manuscripts after Luke 21:38. The style and verbiage is definitely not Johanine.

It is a clever story, similar to the question concerning the tribute to Caesar (Mk 22:13-17 et al) wherein the leaders of the Jews try to trap Jesus with a situation they feel will incriminate him regardless of his response. The Law of Moses, Dt. 23:24, says that a young woman who is caught in the act of adultery is to be stoned. If Jesus allows the stoning he contradicts his own teaching about mercy, whereas if he tells them to let her go he contradicts the Law of Moses. As with the tribute to Caesar, Jesus makes an unexpected response which traps his accusers by making them aware that, as sinners themselves, they have no right to pass judgment on the woman.

## The Fifth Sign—The Man Born Blind (9:1-41)

This miracle narrative may be a continuation of the discussion with the Pharisees found in 8:12-20. As I said above, the content found in Chapters 7 and 8 seems disjointed. Jesus' discussion with "The Jews" from 8:21 to

---

[61] If one continues with the idea of the replacement theme in John one can see in this case how Jesus has replaced Abraham. The Jews were the children of their father, Abraham but if they follow Jesus they are children of his father, God. Along these lines, he also would be seen as replacing Moses in the Bread of Life Discourse (6:22- 71). Moses provided manna in the desert but Jesus provides the "living bread" of which one can eat and possess eternal life.

the end of the Chapter seems to be an insert to address issues that had
arisen between the conservative Jews in John's community and BD over the
divinity of Jesus. The story of the blind man more naturally follows 8:20
especially since Jesus is still in the Temple area when he passes by the man
who is blind from birth.

Notice the question by the disciples in verse 2. The common belief
among the Jews was that blindness, lameness, deafness, etc. was the result
of one's sins and therefore a punishment from God. In the case of someone
being born with such a malady they judged that, since it couldn't be due
to personal sin, it must be because of the sins of his or her parents. Jesus
denies this by saying that his blindness will serve as an opportunity for God
to reveal his glory.

This fifth sign is used to reintroduce or to continue the themes of Jesus
as the "Light of the World" and as the "Living Water". The man's blindness
here probably represents a lack of faith. In a sense, when he "sees" he sees the
light who is Jesus and ultimately believes in him. The healing is accomplished
only after he washes his eyes in the Pool of Siloam. This is the pool from
which the waters were drawn to sprinkle the altar during the Feast. Jesus
has, in a sense, turned that water into life-giving water.

The healing is followed by a continuation of Jesus' conflict with the
Pharisees. A problem has occurred because Jesus "made clay with his saliva
and smeared it on the man's eyes" (9:6). According to the Pharisees, this was
work that was forbidden on the Sabbath. This is compounded by the healing
itself. The question is, "How can someone who willfully breaks Sabbath
Law heal a blind man, especially one who has been blind from birth?" If
the man is blind because of sin then only God or someone sent by God
can cure his blindness. This is the problem that the Pharisees are facing.
At first they try to prove that the man wasn't blind from birth. They even
question his parents who provide guarded answers because as the text says,
"If anyone acknowledges him (Jesus) as the Messiah, he would be expelled
from the synagogue." This is an obvious reflection of the tension between
John's community and the synagogue leaders.

The story ends by contrasting the faith of the blind sinner who now sees,
i.e. believes in Jesus, to the Pharisees who, even though they can physically
see, are blind, i.e. have no faith and, therefore, do not accept Jesus.[62]

---

[62]   Notice the irony here. The Pharisees believe that suffering is the result of sin
and that's why the man was born blind. Contrarily, Jesus says that if they were

## The Good Shepherd (10:1-42)

The narrative about the good shepherd is a continuation of Jesus' attack against the Pharisees in chapter nine. "Amen, amen, I say to you . . ." (10:7) is obviously addressed to them. Throughout the Hebrew Scriptures God is portrayed as a shepherd. The most famous citing is Psalm 23—"The Lord is my shepherd, I shall not want . . .". Many important people in the Hebrew Scriptures were shepherds including Moses and David. Ezekiel 34: says that God will choose a shepherd in the messianic age.

The figures in the good shepherd narrative are allegorical. Jesus is the good shepherd; the Pharisees are the hired hands and the sheep are all those who seek God. Those who follow Jesus are special because they will be given eternal life. Jesus makes it clear that those who follow him are like the blind man. They recognize his voice (9:37-38) and follow him. Later, after Jesus' resurrection, when Mary Magdalene comes to the tomb she thinks Jesus is a gardener until he speaks to her. As soon as he says "Mary" she knows it is Jesus because, as one of those who belong to the sheepfold, she recognizes his voice.

Jesus is the good shepherd because he will lay down his life for his sheep. The hired hands will run away from death—even his followers will do that—but he will willingly accept death for the sake of his sheep. Later, during the Last Supper discourses Jesus will say, "No one has greater love for his friends than to lay down his life for them" (15:13).

Jesus refers to himself as the gate, reminding his listeners that no one can enter the sheepfold, i.e. the Kingdom of God, accept through him. This, of course, echoes 3:16. See the footnote on page 81 regarding this passage.

Jesus refers to "other sheep" (10:16) which either refers to the Gentile communities who have come to believe in him or it might refer to all the churches which do not belong to the community of the Beloved Disciple.[63] As I mentioned earlier, BD believes his community has the truth and all the other churches and "the Jews" have to conform in order to truly possess the truth.

---

innocently blind like the man who was cured they would have no sin, a direct contradiction of the accepted belief. The real problem is that they refuse to recognize that they are spiritually blind and, as such, fail to accept Jesus.

[63] "The Book of Mormon, purportedly received by John Smith from the angle Moroni, refers to this passage. In this case, members of the Church of the Latter-day saints are the "other sheep".

The discourse leads to division, probably reflecting the contemporary divisions both in and outside of BD's community. The main issue is whether Jesus is the Messiah and the discussion is carried over to the conclusion of this chapter. Jesus has obliquely stated he's the Messiah by claiming to be Israel's shepherd. Several times in this Gospel Jesus has made it clear he is God's messenger and, of course, his works, i.e. miracles, are signs that he is the Messiah. Still, they refuse to believe, some so strongly that they "pick up rocks to stone him" (10:31). However, at the end of the chapter, (10:42) we are told again that, "many there began to believe in him."

## The Sixth Sign—The Raising of Lazarus (11:1-57)

The raising of Lazarus is without a doubt, the greatest of Jesus' miracles. It is the longest miracle narrative found in all four Gospels so it is very strange that none of the other Evangelists mention it. Luke 16:19-30 records the well-known story of Lazarus and the rich man. Here, of course, Lazarus is fictitious and is cast as a leper. But there are some similarities. John 11:2 refers to Mary as the one who anointed Jesus, a story which he records in (12:1-8). Both Matthew and Mark record the same anointing which takes place in Bethany at the home of Simon the Leper. Could Simon also be called Lazarus? More on this later. In Luke's story Lazarus dies and while he isn't raised from the dead, the rich man begs Abraham to send Lazarus back to visit his five brothers to warn them that if they don't change their ways eternal torment awaits them. I think there's enough evidence here to suggest that there was a Lazarus tradition that circulated among the first century Churches.[64] Bits and pieces were woven together to form stories but only John appears to have the tradition regarding his resurrection.

---

[64]  A fragment, discovered in 1958, of a previously unknown letter attributed to Clement of Alexandria contains an excerpt from "The Secret Gospel of Mark" which describes a woman from Bethany, whose brother has died. She implores Jesus for mercy and he goes to the tomb, rolls back the stone and raises the youth from the dead. The young man, who is rich, "looks at Jesus with love" and desires to be his follower. There are obvious similarities between this story and John's but Clément's version is much simpler indicating his might be from an earlier source.

John wants to make sure his audience understands that Lazarus is beyond resuscitation, hence the note that he has been dead for four days. The Jews believed that the soul remained in the vicinity of the body for three days. Since it is longer than three days, it is certain that the soul of Lazarus has departed to the land of the dead.[65]

Jesus first encounters Martha, one of Lazarus' two sisters. Both Martha and Mary are mentioned in Luke 10:38-42. Notice Mary remained seated as she was "seated at the feet of Jesus" in Luke 10:39. Martha and Jesus enter into a dialogue about the resurrection of the dead. Martha provides the traditional Pharisaical belief that the dead will rise on the Day of Judgment. Jesus reminds her that he is the source of all life and that those who believe in him will never die which figuratively means that, after death, they will enter into a new and everlasting life.

Martha's response echoes Peter's great confession in the Synoptics when she says, "I believe you are the Messiah, the Son of God . . ." (11:27). As I mentioned earlier, women play an important role in John's Gospel. It is not by accident that Martha has an apostolic role as will Mary Magdalene after the resurrection.

Jesus' next encounter is with Mary. Like Martha she tells him that if he had come earlier her brother would not have died. Jesus then appears to be deeply perturbed, apparently because the women and the "Jews" were weeping. Actually, the literal translation for Jesus' reaction can be interpreted as either, "groaned from within" or "snorted in spirit"! Neither translation makes much sense. Perhaps he is troubled because they still fail to believe that he has the power over life and death. Based on all he has said and the signs he has performed perhaps, he feels they should believe he has the power to bring Lazarus back to life.

When Jesus asks to have the stone removed, Mary's response, "Surly there will be a stench!" reinforces John's premise than Lazarus' spirit has completely left him. Jesus' prayer to his Father reminds the crowd that all his power comes from God.

When Lazarus comes forth from the tomb he is bound with linen strips such that he needed to be untied to allow him to move. I believe John is using this image to demonstrate that Jesus has not only freed Lazarus from

---

[65] This place was called *Sheol*, and ancient Hebrew term for the underworld. It originally designated a place of confinement but not punishment; a place where the soul aimlessly exists until the Last Judgment.

the power of death but also from sin, the consequence which, according to Genesis 2:17, is death. Therefore, Lazarus was healed both in body and in spirit.

John uses the resurrection of Lazarus to prefigure Jesus' own resurrection. Notice how the tomb in which Lazarus is buried in like the tomb in which Jesus is buried; the cloths that wrapped Lazarus were similar to the grave clothes of Jesus. In essence, the resurrection of Lazarus is the revelation of Jesus' mission and purpose—that he comes from the Father, he is the revelation of the Father and he is the resurrection and the life. This will ultimately be revealed when he, like Lazarus, dies and is raised to life. The difference will be that, unlike Lazarus, he will not have to die again and unlike Lazarus his death and resurrection will be salvific.

Chapter 11 concludes with the chief priests and the Pharisees conspiring with the High Priest to have Jesus put to death. John tells us that because of this miracle many came to believe in Jesus but now his enemies are convinced that he must die. This miracle was the last straw for them.

This is different from the Synoptic versions, of which all three Gospels claim the cleansing of the Temple was the precipitating event that convinced the leaders to put Jesus to death. John moved the cleansing of the Temple to near the beginning of his Gospel and replaced it with the Lazarus narrative. He did this because he wanted the signs to increase in power building to a crescendo of convincing proof that Jesus was who he said he was.

## The Anointing at Bethany and the Conclusion of the Book of Signs (12:1-50)

This story is found in all four Gospels. Matthew and Mark's version is very similar to John's pericope while Luke is somewhat different both in content and purpose. Matthew, Mark and John say that the anointing took place within the week before Passover. Luke places it during a time when John the Baptizer was still alive. All, except Luke's version, take place in Bethany, however, Matthew and Mark say that the scene occurs in the home of Simon the leper rather than the home of Lazarus. Luke does not tell us the name of the town but says the anointing took place in the home of a Pharisee whose name is also Simon (Luke7:16-50). Only John tells us the woman is Mary the sister of Lazarus. All four accounts mention the woman used expensive ointment; Mark and John say it was nard. In Matthew and Mark the woman anoints Jesus' head ( a sign that he is the Messiah) whereas Luke and John say she anointed his feet and dried them with her hair. In all the accounts there are complaints that the money used to purchase the ointment could have been given to the poor. Only John says it was Judas who complained, not because he cared for the poor but because "he was a thief"(12:6). All the narratives say the ointment was worth 300 days wages.

It's obvious that all four stories are derived from a single incident. Luke uses his version to introduce and explain Jesus' attitude regarding forgiveness. Here, the woman is cast as a prostitute. Jesus uses the incident to relay a parable about two people who are in debt to a creditor, one for a larger sum the other for a small sum. He demonstrates that the one who is forgiven the greatest debt will love the one who forgave him more than the other.[66] So too will the sinful woman be forgiven because she has shown great love for Jesus by washing his feet and perfuming them with oil.

Even though Matthew and Mark have many more similarities to John than Luke, I believe Luke is much closer to John than meets the eye. While Mary, the sister of Lazarus is not cast as a prostitute her actions betray that of a sinful woman. Like the prostitute in Luke, Mary lets her hair hang down freely and, as in Luke's version wipes Jesus' feet with her hair. Respectful women of that time never let their hair down in public. The woman in Luke loved much; Mary is described as one whom Jesus loved. Furthermore, prostitutes used perfumed oil as part of their trade. The description in both Luke and John's version is sensual.

Because Mary Magdalene appears shortly after this scene in Luke's Gospel she was erroneously identified with the woman; hence she was historically cast as a prostitute. However, Mary Magdalene is definitely not Mary the sister of Lazarus nor was she a prostitute.[67]

Why does John seem to cast Mary as a woman of ill repute? Perhaps she was a repentant prostitute. She, like her sister, seems not to have a husband. While I don't think she had an intimate relationship with Jesus, as a former prostitute, it may have been natural for her to show affection and/or devotion in this way.

---

[66]   Often the word debt can mean sin. For example, the RSV translates Matthew 6:12, "Forgive us our debts as we have forgiven our debtors." Hence the example given here by Jesus is obviously about forgiving sin rather than a sum of money.

[67]   Mk 15:4 says that Mary Magdalene followed and provided for Jesus when he was in Galilee. Bethany, the home of Lazarus and his sisters was in Judea.

Certainly, there is a connection between her anointing Jesus' feet and Jesus washing the feet of his disciples in 13:1-20. Mary is a true servant and a true disciple because she performs her act of service before Jesus provocatively demonstrates that true discipleship means to serve others even in the most menial way.

Unlike the Synoptic versions, John uses this story to prepare for Jesus' triumphal entry into Jerusalem. The Synoptics place the anointing after the entry into Jerusalem. They also indicate that the entry was staged by Jesus and the disciples whereas in John it is a spontaneous occurrence orchestrated by those who witnessed or heard about the raising of Lazarus from the dead.

Like the Synoptic versions Jesus remains in Jerusalem preaching in the Temple area although in John's version Jesus has been in Jerusalem for some time. For Matthew, Mark and Luke this is the first and only time Jesus comes to Jerusalem and then only for what we now call Holy Week.

Verses 20-50 summarize the basic teachings found in the Book of Signs. Jesus reminds the people that his hour has come, i.e. the time for his suffering and death. This "hour" will be the final proof that he is everything he has said he is. 12:27-28 is similar to Jesus' words spoken in the Agony in the Garden described by the Synoptics except that here Jesus willfully accepts death without question.

The chapter concludes with Jesus' proclamation that he is the light, the revelation of God and that belief in him leads to eternal life.


## THE BOOK OF GLORY (13:1-20:31)

The basic theme of the Book of Glory is found in the opening verse. Here we are told Jesus knows that his hour, i.e. his suffering, death and resurrection, is upon him and that he must return to his Father. He will prove true to his mission by showing his love for his disciples and he will love them even, or perhaps especially, by dying for them. The theme echoes the words found in the prologue, "But to those who did accept him he gave the power to become children of God, to those who believe in his name, who were born, not by natural generation nor by human choice nor by a man's decision but by God." (1:13-13)

As with the Synoptics, the events of Chapter 13-18 take place in the context of a meal but as I mentioned earlier, unlike the Synoptic description, it is not a Passover meal. John 13:1 says, "Before the feast of Passover . . ."

and John 19:31 tells us that Jesus was crucified on the Day of Preparation which is the day before Passover.

One cannot be sure who was present at this meal. If the Beloved Disciple is Lazarus as I contend, then the attendees were not limited to the Twelve. Some of the Twelve are mentioned by name but John refers to all who are present as "the disciples" which could include followers other than the Twelve. It does not appear that there are any women present.


## The Washing of the Disciples' Feet (13:2-20)

Certainly, this is one of the most provocative scenes in the Gospels. Jesus, their Lord and Master, who, according to John, is the same as God, kneels down and performs the most menial of tasks. The foot washing appears to take the place of the institution of the Eucharist found in all three of the other Gospels.

Washing feet was rarely demanded of a slave. It was often meted out to slaves as a punishment. In the Greco-Roman world feet were considered disgusting. Sandals did not protect one's feet from the elements. They were dirty and often infected with sores and disease. People in first century Palestine washed their own feet. That's why Peter was so upset. He couldn't stand to see his Master demean himself in this way.

Yet, Jesus washes not only the feet of those who loved him; he also washes Judas' feet! His actions remind us of the words of Paul in Philippians, "Who, though he was in the form of God did not regard equality with God something to be grasped. Rather he emptied himself taking the form of a slave" (Phil 2:6-7). 13:13, "whoever has bathed . . ." appears to have a baptismal connotation. They have been purified by the waters of baptism; now they need to understand what it means to be a disciple, i.e. to live out one's baptismal promises.

Jesus tells his disciples that they must do as he has done. He has given them an example. The true disciple is not just a servant but a slave! He or she not only obeys and serves the Master but also one another even when the other is a peon so to speak. It seems to me that Church leaders have never gotten this message. Most see themselves as people of privilege and the higher they are on the ecclesial ladder, the more privilege they command. Sadly, while they may read the Gospel they don't seem to really hear it.

## The Last Discourse (13:31-17:26)

After Jesus announces his betrayal and Judas leaves he begins his farewell speech. We find this kind of speech in the Hebrew Scriptures and in Jewish apocryphal literature. Jacob gives his farewell address to his children in Gen. 49:2-27, Moses to Israel in Deut. 33:2-29 and Joshua to Israel in Josh. 23-24:2-24. The *Testaments of the Twelve Patriarchs*, a psuedepigraphic text written between 100 **BCE** and 100 **CE,** contains a literary form that is very similar to the discourses found in John 13-17.

Jesus starts by giving the Disciples a "new commandment", one which tells them they must love one another as he has loved them. As they must serve as he serves so also they must love as he loves. The statement is very sectarian. It is not like Matthew 5:44 which says they must love their enemies and pray for their persecutors. John's Jesus says they must "love *one another*" (italics mine). As I said earlier, John's Gospel is very sectarian. One is either "in" or "out". If you are out, you are lost. Only the "in crowd" are the true children of God and deserving of God's love and the love of each other. John's Jesus never prays for the world. He only prays for his own (17:9) and his own, though in the world, do not belong to the world (17:14-15).

Chapters 14-17 divide the discourse into three parts. The first part (Chapter 14) continues to stress the theme of his departure and focuses on the new role of the Holy Spirit who is called the Paraclete.[68] This advocate will remain with them after Jesus leaves to empower them to keep his commandments and teach them everything they need to know about Jesus (14:26) He is the Spirit of peace and will give them peace. It is not the peace that the world offers, in this case Shalom, but the peace that comes from knowing salvation belongs to all those who believe in Jesus.

The second division (Chaps. 15 & 16) is repetitive and probably was added by one of the editors.[69] It repeats the commandment to "love one

---

[68]  Normally the Greek word for spirit in the New Testament is *pneuma*. However in the Last Supper discourses John's Jesus uses the word *paracletos* which means advocate or councilor. In this sense the Spirit will defend his followers much like a public defender in a court of law.

[69]  Chapter 14 ends with the words, "Get up, let us go" (14:31) which implies that chapters 15 -17 were added by an editor. Chapter 18 begins with the words, "When he had said this, Jesus went out with his disciples across the Kidron valley…" which sounds like the normal transition from 14:31.

another" and speaks of the world's hatred of Jesus and his disciples and again describes the role of the Holy Spirit. The section about the vine and the branches (15:1-10) is pure allegory. Israel was often portrayed in the Hebrew Scriptures as God's vineyard. In this case Jesus is talking about the New Israel, the kingdom that he is ushering in. Jesus has replaced those Israelite leaders who have been in charge of the vineyard. He is the "true vine" and God is the vine grower (15:1). All those who believe in Jesus, i.e. attached to the vine, will inherit this new Israel. They will remain in him and in his love (and therefore attached to the vine) if they keep his commandment to love one another. Since they are attached to the vine they are part of him and belong to him. "The World" is all those outside the community. They have rejected Jesus and therefore, are rejected by him. The chapter ends with a reminder that the disciples will suffer for the sake of the Gospel and with a reiteration of the promise to send the Advocate (16:26)

The third and final division contains the "Priestly Prayer" of Jesus. Here he prays for his own glorification, for those the Father has given him and for those who believe in him because of the witness of his disciples. It is one of the few times we actually hear the words of Jesus at prayer. However, it is highly doubtful that Jesus ever said these words in the flesh. The prayer certainly wouldn't have been recorded when it was said and the theology is too far advanced. This is the prayer of the risen Lord Jesus spoken through the prophet(s) of BD's community.

The first part of the prayer (17:1-8) focuses on Jesus' relationship with the Father. It repeats John's themes that Jesus is the revelation of God, that he has glorified the Father through his works and that he is the source of everlasting life.

The second part (9-19) focuses on the disciples. He consecrates them and asks the Father to protect them from the world which now clearly represents the realm of evil. He doesn't ask God to take them out of this world (a typical Gnostic belief) but to protect them as he protected them while he was on earth. This, of course would be the work of the Advocate.

The third and final part (17:20-26) focuses on future believers. He prays that they too will be one in him as he is in the Father and as his disciples are in him. This theme is an obvious carry-over from the vine and branches allegory. It also may be a reflection on the division that already exists in John's community. Unity is a principle work of the Holy Spirit and it is unity among all believers that Jesus desires. How sad it is that he has never gotten his wish.

## The Passion and Death of Jesus

John's passion follows the same outline as Mark beginning with Jesus' arrest, followed by the trial before the High Priest, then Pilate and finally the crucifixion, death and burial. However, John's version has several differences. Perhaps the biggest difference is the day of crucifixion. The Synoptics state that Jesus is crucified on the day of Passover; John says that it's the day before known as the Day of Preparation. Obviously, one account is wrong and the other is right. Most likely, John has conveniently changed the day to fit his theme that Jesus is "the lamb of God who takes away the sins of the world"(1:29). The Day of Preparation was the day that the priests slaughtered the lambs for the Passover feast. He even notes that this day is the preparation day and that it was about noon when he was crucified. The lambs were typically slaughtered at noon.

Some of the other differences between John and the Synoptics are as follows:

1) Jesus knows Judas is coming and goes out to meet him (18:4).
2) Jesus is not questioned by the Sanhedrin, only by Annas and Caiaphas (18:19-24).
3) Peter is taken to the courtyard by BD because he is known to the High Priest (18:15)
4) Pilate desperately tries to release Jesus and appeals to the crowd three times and, after questioning Jesus, is portrayed as being afraid of him (18:28-19:16)
5) The women are close to the crucifixion scene as opposed to being far of in the distance in the Synoptics (19:25).
6) Jesus has a conversation with his mother and the Beloved Disciple who are standing at the foot of the Cross (19:26-27).
7) A soldier pierces the side of Jesus with a lance causing a flow of water and blood 19:34).
8) Nicodemus, apparently a disciple, accompanies Joseph of Arimathea for the burial and the text implies that Jesus' body is anointed and then wrapped with the burial cloths.[70]

---

[70] The Shroud of Turin shows a body that was not washed or anointed. However, the arms appear to be tied and there seems to be a chin band to keep the mouth closed and, of course the shroud which covered the body.

The major difference between John and the Synoptics is that John's Jesus orchestrates his passion and is in total control. In the Synoptics, especially Mark, he is at the mercy of his captors; he is afraid, he feels abandoned and suffers terribly. John's Jesus has no fear of dying and almost appears not to suffer. The cross is his "hour". It is the final hour. He is lifted up as the serpent was lifted up in the desert which fulfilled his promise that through his death all people will be drawn to him (12:32). The cross is his throne. He is the king who now reigns over the whole world. The inscription written above the cross in three languages (19:20) testifies this is true. This is the seventh and final sign which ultimately reveals who he really is. If they don't understand it now they probably never will.

The water which flows from his side symbolizes baptism and the Holy Spirit,[71] the two ways to gain entrance into the Kingdom of God, a kingdom made available because of his suffering and death. Jesus' final words, "It is finished." (19:30) reminds us that he is still in charge even in death. Notice he doesn't "give up his spirit" as in the Synoptics; rather he hands it over.

Everything has now been fulfilled. The journey is over. The final hour has come and Jesus is the victor, as are all who believe in him.

## The Resurrection Narratives (20:1-21:25)

There are two chapters of resurrection stories. The first, Chapter 20, is part of the original Gospel and only contains appearances which take place in Jerusalem. The second, Chapter 21, is an obvious addition. The literally style is more Lucan than Johanine. The narrator refers to the Beloved Disciple in the third person and even says this Gospel is the testimony of BD (21:24). In this chapter Jesus appears to seven of the disciples in Galilee.

Jesus first appears to Mary Magdalene (20:11-18). This contradicts Luke who states that it was Peter or the two on the road to Emmaus (Lk 24:13-35) and Paul who also says it was Peter (1 Cor 15:4). As I mentioned earlier, women play a predominant role in John's Gospel.

---

[71]   The blood could also symbolize the Eucharist; however, since there is no institution of the Eucharist in John I doubt that this is the case. The focus throughout the Gospel has been baptism and the Holy Spirit. "No one can enter the Kingdom of God without being born of water and Spirit (3:5).

At first, Mary doesn't recognize Jesus, perhaps a sign that only believers can see the risen Lord. Like the two on the road to Emmaus, she too has lost her faith because the LAW said Jesus became a curse when he was crucified. However, once Jesus calls her by name, she recognizes him. He is the good shepherd and his sheep know his voice (10:3). She most likely fell down and grasped his feet, a typical gesture for a female disciple, but is warned by Jesus not to hold onto him. It is also Jesus' way of saying that he is not going to remain with them in the flesh. Mary is then commissioned to tell the disciples that he has risen. She will indeed become an apostle to the apostles, the first one to spread the good news that Jesus was raised from the dead. How strange that some churches still don't allow the ordination of women even when the Christian Scriptures make it clear that some were apostles, others were teachers and still others deaconesses.[72]

The only other recorded appearance in this chapter takes place in a room in Jerusalem. It was probably the same room where the last supper was celebrated. Jesus appears to the disciples behind closed doors. The fact that Jesus can enter the room when all the doors are locked indicates that he now has a different body. Notice it is in this upper room on Easter Sunday that he gives the disciples the Holy Spirit. This, of course, contradicts Acts 2:1-13. Notice that Jesus breathes on them which is reminiscent of God breathing life into Adam. As God gave Adam corporal life so now Jesus gives his disciples spiritual life.

However, Thomas is absent. When Thomas is told that Jesus appeared to the disciples he recites his now well-known words, "Unless I see the mark of the nails in his hands and put my finger into the nail marks and my hand into his side I will not believe" (20:25). Thomas gets his chance and cries out, "My Lord and my God" (20:28). This story is John's way of pointing out to the Docetists that Jesus was more than just a spirit even after he was raised. One cannot put his fingers in the wounds of a ghost.

The first and only resurrection appearance in chapter 21 takes place in Galilee. This is probably an attempt by the editor to verify Mark 16:7 which said Jesus would appear to the disciples in Galilee. However, it also

---

72    Matt. 28:8 tells us that the women who came to the tomb reported the
      resurrection to the disciples as does Luke 24:9. Priscilla, along with her
      husband Aquila, accompanied Paul as co-workers for the sake of the Gospel
      (Rom. 16:3) and explained the Gospel to Apollos (Acts18:26). Paul mentions
      Phoebe in Rom. 16:1 calling her a Deaconess who has greatly helped him and
      the Church.

provides a lead-in to a serious discussion between Peter and Jesus regarding Peter's role as the principle head of the Church.

The large catch of fish is reminiscent of the pre-resurrection stories found in Mt 14:28-31 and Luke 5:1-11. The number, 153, most likely is symbolic. St Jerome claimed that it was the number of species of fish catalogued by Greek zoologists. Soon the disciples will be catching men instead of fish.

Notice that Jesus already has fish cooking on a charcoal fire. The meal probably symbolizes the Eucharistic. When they finished this meal Jesus takes Peter aside and three times asks him if he loves him and after each of Peter's responses he says, "Feed my sheep." The key to understanding this exchange is found in the Greek text. There are four words for love in New Testament Greek. John's Jesus uses two of them, *philia* and *agape*. *Philia* means brotherly love whereas *agape* means divine love. The first two times Jesus uses the word agape. In other words, "Peter, do you love me *as God loves me?*" Peter responds with the words, "Yes, Lord, you know that I love you *as a brother.*" After Peter responds in this way twice Jesus changes the word for love from *agape* to *philia*. The point that John is making here is that Peter's love for Jesus is imperfect which is evidenced by the fact the he denied Jesus three times. However, the day will come when Peter will again have the opportunity to show his love for Jesus and this time it will be made perfect by dying for him. " . . . when you grow old you will stretch out your hands, and someone else will dress you and lead you where you do not want to go" (21:18).

The chapter ends with the implication that there was a belief in the community that the Beloved Disciple would not die until Jesus came in glory. He obviously has died which disturbed the community. As I mentioned in the beginning of this chapter, why would anyone believe that someone would not die unless he had already died and was raised up? Hence, my belief that Lazarus is BD.

The Gospel ends with the editor saying that BD is responsible for its contents. This does not mean that he wrote all of its words but rather that he was the underlying source.

# JOHN'S JESUS

Human and Divine

John makes it absolutely clear Jesus is divine. He is the pre-existent Word who is one with the Father and who was present with the Father at the beginning of time (1:1:2). He, as the Word of God, is responsible for the creation of the universe (1:4). He is indeed the Son of God, not in the context of being the king of the Jews but as God's divine son. Often he refers to himself using the "I AM" formula (8:24, 28, 58; 13:19) which is part of the Hebrew word Yahweh, the name God gave to Moses.

However, he is also a man. This is a true paradox. He is the Word of God who literally, "pitched his tent with us" (1:14). Even though he knows everything that is going to happen in his life, he still needs to eat and drink like us, he has close friendships and he grieves over the death of Lazarus, even to the point of weeping. He has a real body, one that can be held onto and one that can be pierced with nails and a spear.

This dual nature of Jesus is the foundation of the Church's teaching that he has two natures, human and divine, which are somehow mysteriously linked to one divine person.

Still, he is not a man like Mark's Jesus. He does not get tired, he is never afraid and he apparently doesn't seem to suffer. He does die but it is a death that he wills and controls.

## The Revelation of the Father

Over and over John's Jesus reminds his listeners that when he speaks God is speaking. His words are literally God's words. Everything he says comes from the Father. His words and deeds reveal the Father (6:36). He is the "bread come down from heaven" (6:32-36) which provides food for the soul and replaces the Torah. Those who see him through the eyes of faith see the Father (14:9). Everything he does appears to be orchestrated by the Father. He has been given authority by the Father to bring judgment upon the world (6:27) and to overcome the darkness of sin in the world.

## The Son of Man

Jesus refers to himself as the Son of Man for the first time during his conversation with Nicodemus (3:13). This is an eschatological title, found in all the Gospels, for the apocalyptic figure in the Book of Daniel. It is paradoxical in John because Jesus is presented far more as Savior than judge.

However, because he is the light of world he will expose the darkness of sin and evil in the world which will demand judgment. The Father has given him the authority to judge (6:22) but his judgment is reserved solely to those who reject him. Still, Jesus desires to save the world far more than to condemn it; so much so that he sent the Advocate to teach and defend the believer. Ultimately, judgment will come at the end of the world.

## The Light of the World

In the very beginning of this Gospel we are told the Word who is Jesus is the light which has come into the world, a light that shines in the darkness of sin (1:5-6). John the Baptizer testified to the light (1:6) and Jesus is the true light who enlightens everyone (1:9). Even though there are those who prefer darkness (3:19) all those who prefer the light will walk in the light (8:12) and if they believe they will become children of the light (12:36). This concept of light and darkness is often found in the Qumran scrolls. Light here and in the Gospels always represents goodness and truth. Pilate asks Jesus, "What is truth?" Jesus has already told him that he came into the world to testify to the truth which means everything that comes from God. But this truth can only be understood by those who have come out of the darkness and into the light—the light who is Christ.

## Conclusion

John presents a Jesus who, in many ways, is completely different than the Jesus found in the Synoptic Gospels. Rather than the son of Mary he is the risen Lord, who was and is the pre-existent Logos united to God since the beginning of time. While he was born of a woman he is far more than a man, far greater than any of the prophets and far greater than angels. He is the divine Son of the Father through whom everything came into being. As such, he is the revelation of God. Everything he says and does reveals the Father. He always does the Father's will; he even sends the Spirit of God into the world. His light of truth shines in the darkness of this sinful world so that the people of the world can hear and believe in the Truth, a belief that brings everlasting life. He is the God-man who has brought salvation to the world.

## PERSONAL REFLECTION

When I read about Jesus washing his disciples' feet (13:1-20) it, ironically, stirs up anger inside me. I say this because those who are leaders in the Church, especially those who call themselves the Princes of the Church almost never wash feet. They wear fancy clothes, demand that others show them reverence, kiss their rings and call them Eminence or Excellency. They ride around in limos and live in mansions. They hang around the rich and famous. Instead of being servants, they have servants. How different they are than Jesus. Jesus tells us that the Son of Man has no place to lay his head. He had one seamless garment to wear. He hung around with prostitutes and sinners. And yes, he knelt down and washed his disciples' feet.

Do all these leaders not hear this story? "If I, therefore, the master and teacher, have washed your feet, you ought to wash one another's feet. I have given you a model to follow, so that as I have done for you, you should also do (John 13:14-15).

This statement is not directed to the lowly or even to the everyday disciple although even they must also listen. It is directed to the Twelve Apostles, the ones who would lead the Church, grow the Church and define the Church. Yet those who follow in their footsteps rarely, if ever, kneel down and bathe the sick and the infirmed or cradle the head of a dying man. The Mother Theresa's do that. Nurses do that. Husbands do that for their wives and wives for their husbands, parents for their children . . .

Did not Jesus say that the last will be first and the first will be last? Did he not say, "If you want to be the greatest you must first be the least"? He told the rich man to sell everything he had and give it to the poor before he could become his disciple. Do any of these princes, Tele-evangelists, wealthy Pastors, Ministers and Deacons really hear any of these words? Sadly, most don't.

The main message of this story and the other passages I've quoted is that disciples of Christ must be humble. "Blessed are the meek." If we truly dare to call ourselves Christians then we must be humble servants. Humility is not parading around in fancy robes, wearing Rolex watches, telling others how important we are or how much money we have. It's not about riding around in expensive cars or preaching the Gospel of prosperity or self-discovery. It's about washing feet!

It's easy for me to poke fun at these people and judge them because I'm not one of them. Or am I? How often do I put my needs ahead of others? How often do I brag about my accomplishments or swell up with pride when someone compliments me? Do I tell people how often I pray or go to Church or do works of charity? Do I look out for number one most of the time? It's easy to judge others but we're all Pharisees at times.

The bottom line is that we need to cast off whatever is hindering us from washing feet—no matter whose feet they are or how many times they need to be washed. God give me the vision to see and understand that and the will to do it.

# EPILOGUE

In this book I have tried to show that the Gospels are not words cast in stone but an expression of the Word of God which is Jesus. Below are some of the main points I tried to make:

1.) The Gospels are not the life of Jesus nor are they biographical. While they contain both historical and biographical information they are more about the meaning of the Jesus event, an event that is not limited to Jesus in the flesh. The Holy Spirit, which is in essence the way Jesus continued and continues to be present to the Church, revealed a lot of the material we find in the Gospels, most especially in the Gospel of John. This revelation was primarily given to the prophets within the first century Christian communities and it is the revelation of the Risen Christ. So the Gospels are as much or more about the teachings of the risen Jesus than Jesus of Nazareth.

2.) The Gospels took shape, at least in their present form, over a somewhat lengthy period of time. They began, initially, as an oral tradition. Then, as the number of communities grew and became more diverse, a basic written tradition probably developed. At first, these written documents may have been missionary manuals which recorded a passion narrative and some of the sayings of Jesus. Most likely there were simpler versions of all four of the Gospels. These were redacted and edited over time until they became the Matthew, Mark, Luke and John that we have today. The most import thing to remember is that the Gospels were a work in progress and probably changed somewhat with the changing demands of their respective communities.

3.) Each Gospel was mostly the product of a particular first century Christian community. The given community had issues which needed to be addressed. While we are not certain which community produced a given Gospel there is enough internal evidence to indicate that Mark was written to the Roman Christians who were persecuted by the Emperor Nero Caesar. It's main purpose was to demonstrate the meaning of true discipleship and to show that even the Twelve were weak of faith, deserters and betrayers just like the Roman Christians. These Christians suffered a great deal from the first major persecution of a Church community. However, Jesus suffered as much or more than any of them and because he was faithful to God, he was rewarded with a resurrection to a new life. Because he was raised, so too will his faithful followers be raised.

Another example is John's Gospel which may have been the product of more than one Christian community. His Gospel was directed to several groups of believers, who according the evangelist or evangelists, had strayed from the true teaching which the author(s) possessed. In order to overcome these errant teachings, John tried to convince his readers that Jesus was the Divine Word of God. When Jesus spoke it was God speaking through him and so his words were the direct revelation of God. Jesus was the true and only son of God that always did his Father's will and revealed that will to the community. As a result, those who heard this revelation had to follow it because it came directly from God. There were no options but to believe and obey.

Matthew's objective was to portray Jesus as a new Moses and the greatest of all the prophets, even greater than angels, who re-defined the Law of Moses. His community appears to have been persecuted by the Pharisees who, after the destruction of Jerusalem, saw themselves as the new interpreters of the Law of Moses. Matthew's Jesus stands up to these Pharisees and shows them to be hypocrites and corrupters of the spirit of the LAW which, according to Matthew, has to do with mercy and love far more than justice.

Luke was a compiler of sources. He/she pieced together all the sources which were available by the early part of the second century to show the tremendous growth of the Church—from its humble beginnings in Bethlehem to St Paul freely preaching the Gospel in Rome, the center of the known world. His community was either very poor or very wealthy. I believe it's the latter. He is trying to demonstrate that one cannot buy their way into heaven, that wealth and status have little or no value in the Kingdom of Heaven. The true Christian is humble and obedient to the will of God. Using these criteria, even the outcasts and the marginalized in society can have a free ticket to paradise.

4.) The world of the first Christians and the events of the first century Greco-Roman world had a great deal of influence on the content of the Gospels. Sectarian groups of Jews as well as religious structures were underlying forces. The Essenes, Gnostic Jews and Christians, Synagogue structure and leadership, the followers of John the Baptist as well as his teachings are but a few of these forces. The entire structure of the household churches was patterned after the synagogue especially before the destruction of Jerusalem. The teaching of John the Baptist as well as his practice of baptism was continued by Jesus and the disciples who followed Jesus. The Essenes certainly influenced John the Baptist and his followers. Some of these followers became disciples of Jesus and their thoughts and beliefs were brought into the early Church. The caste system, which was prevalent in Palestine, became one of the main targets of Jesus' teaching. The treatment of woman as though they were property was condemned by Jesus, probably more so in real life than what we see in the Gospels but it is certainly there. Jewish festivals were important to Jesus and served as an opportunity for him to spread the Gospel not just to the poor but also to the wealthy and those who came to these feasts from far-off places. Sacrificial offerings in the Temple and the Temple itself provided a backdrop for many Gospel stories. So, a cultural understanding of Palestine and even the first century Greco-Roman world is an important part of understanding the Gospel message.

5.) While I think it's important to study the Scripture, especially the Gospels, it's also important to read them reflectively. That's why I added the reflections at the end of each Gospel. I hope I have given you an idea of what I mean by reflecting on the words or passages of the Gospels. Reflection doesn't require a lot of knowledge, only the knowledge the Holy Spirit shares with you via prayerful contemplation. A word of caution. You need to be sure that what you are hearing is coming from the Spirit. The rule I use is that if what I am hearing is not leading me to be more loving, more forgiving, more open to the needs of others plus a greater longing for God, then it is not from the Holy Spirit.

I hope that you have enjoyed reading this book as much as I have enjoyed writing it. I hope you have learned a great deal about the Gospels but most of all I hope that it has helped to bring you closer to God and God's people.

November 1, 2010. The Feast of All Saints

CPSIA information can be obtained at www.ICGtesting.com
Printed in the USA
BVOW042333051211

277651BV00005B/45/P